HEALING RAYS

BY

PRINCIPAL GEORGE JEFFREYS
(Founder and Leader of the Elim Foursquare Gospel Alliance)

London :

ELIM PUBLISHING COMPANY, LIMITED,
PARK CRESCENT, CLAPHAM, S.W.4.

First published in March, 1932

MADE AND PRINTED IN GREAT BRITAIN
BY THE ELIM PUBLISHING COMPANY, LTD., LONDON

Kessinger Publishing's Rare Reprints
Thousands of Scarce and Hard-to-Find Books!

-
-
-
-
-
-
-
-
-
-
-
-
-
-
-
-
-
-

We kindly invite you to view our extensive catalog list at:
http://www.kessinger.net

HEALING RAYS

PRINCIPAL GEORGE JEFFREYS
Founder and Leader
of the
Elim Foursquare Gospel Alliance

PUBLISHERS' NOTE

THE unique position which Principal George Jeffreys holds in the religious life of the British Isles is sufficient reason why his book is being added to the large number already published on the subject of Divine healing. He is the founder and leader of the most remarkable revival and healing movement of latter years—a movement that has won tens of thousands to the Saviour and brought healing through the Name of Christ to multitudes of sick folk. The author has pioneered the combined message of Salvation, Healing, Baptism of the Holy Ghost and the Second Advent of Christ in the largest and most historic halls, including the Royal Albert Hall and the Crystal Palace in London, and the Bingley Exhibition Hall in Birmingham, pictures of which appear in this book. These great auditoriums have been packed to overflowing with monster congregations in the grip of Holy Ghost revival. The many astonishing testimonies of those who have been miraculously healed in the great gatherings have received world-wide publicity through the medium of the secular press. The vacant spinal carriages and bath chairs, the discarded crutches, the cast-off steel and other kinds of body jackets, the cripples who now walk, the cancer and tumour cases that have been miraculously healed, all eloquently testify to the supernatural character of his ministry. The author of this book, having ministered to the sick for a period of seventeen years after being healed himself, writes with unequivocal authority. He has not submitted abstract theories but concrete facts—facts that have been demonstrated with phenomenal success in his great ministry of revival and healing.

CONTENTS

Contents

Contents

of healing accelerated—Mixture of grace and
works—King Asa and curative means—
Healings : do they last?—Claim victory over
death—Paul's thorn an argument for Divine
healing—" Signs an evidence that faith is
lacking "—Not all healed—Failure attributable to lack of faith—Revival and healing
campaigns—Steps leading to healing—Be
sure you are in line with God's will—Be
sure to obey the commandments of God—
Remember the Lord's death—Bring tithes
into storehouse—Confess any wrongdoing to
those you have injured—Hindrances in the
way of healing—Unbelief—Seeking healing
for self-gratification—Being guilty of personal sins—Modes of healing—Direct appeal
on part of individual—Co-operation and
fellowship of practical sympathisers—Co-
operation and mutual fellowship of prayer-
warriors—Laying-on of hands—Anointing
with oil—Going forth of God's Word—
Ministry of prayer in the Church—Things
to remember when seeking healing—See that
spiritual life is nourished by prayer and
reading of God's Word—Healing, like salvation, is of grace ; therefore do not consider
your own worthiness—Do not worry over
little faith—Do not be overburdened about
your long-standing disease—Do not be discouraged if not immediately healed—Due
attention must be given to laws of health,
etc.—A cheerful heart is a tonic to yourself
and to others—God is glorified and His
works made manifest when the supernatural
is in evidence.

Contents

in the past always seems a greater wonder
—Ordinary human channels of to-day nothing
like the great men of the past—Under-
estimation of Holy Ghost operations—Remarkable testimonies of the healed who have
stood the test of years—Healed of insanity
—Helpless cripple healed—Another cripple
healed—Sleeping sickness, blindness and
seizure healed—Cured of epileptic fits—
Cancer rooted out by the power of God—
Fractured knee-cap healed—Dilated stomach
healed—Baptist minister's wife healed of
cancer—Another cripple healed—Healed of
St. Vitus' dance—Skin disease healed—
Another cripple delivered—Another bath-
chair case healed—Growth disappears—
Healed of rupture—Another cripple healed—
A thankful mother's testimony—*Ministry of
the Miraculous*—John Leech, M.A., K.C.,
LL.B., on the Revival and Healing Move-
ment—Viewpoint of Rev. Professor Cunning-
Ham Pike, M.A.

HEALING RAYS

*But unto you that fear My Name shall the
Sun of Righteousness arise with healing in
His wings (or rays—Moffatt)—Malachi iv. 2.*

Healing rays! Yes, they radiate from our
Lord and Saviour Jesus Christ, the glorious
Sun of Righteousness. We have been con-
scious of them as we have ministered in His
Name, and have come under their vivifying,
health-giving and invigorating properties.
The warmth of the spiritual calorific ray has
driven away the coldness of unbelief, and the
transforming effect of the actinic has resulted
in changed lives and homes. The light that
comes from Christ not only illuminates and
beautifies the soul, it gives health and vigour
to the mortal body. Under the powerful
influence of His spiritual rays we have seen
the weak grow strong, the diseased made
whole and the barren life become fruitful.
We have seen them steal through the avenues
of faith until the weakened frame has been
quickened and healed. This book on healing simply contains the subject matter of our
studies and addresses during seventeen years'
ministry in revival and healing campaigns,
put into book form in response to requests
that have been increasing each year.

HEALING RAYS

CHAPTER I

Bodily Healing
Introductory—Explanatory

THE subject of bodily healing is evidently claiming the attention of Christendom, and there is a widespread desire to know the truth respecting this most important theme. It has brought forth volumes from the pens of able writers, some relegating all miracles of healing to a past dispensation, while others postpone them to the coming Millennium. It has also become a theme for discussion in most theological colleges, and the Scriptures are being searched with new earnestness and purpose. The one great reason why it is dominating the mind of the public is the fact that thousands are bearing testimonies to bodily healings. They claim to have been miraculously healed in answer to prayer under the ministry of the laying-on of hands or the anointing with oil, as people were in Bible days. These manifestations of healing are not confined to the British Isles, they are being experienced over the whole world. Everywhere deliverances from deadly diseases are avowed, and miracles are being wrought, the

1

replicas of which can only be found in the Bible. Neither are they exclusively experienced by any one particular sect or community that holds bodily healing as one of its tenets of belief, but by spiritual ministers, evangelists and church workers of all denominations. The method of procedure in ministering to the sick is not always the same. Some evangelists are called upon to lay hands publicly, and vast congregations have witnessed astounding miracles, others anoint the sick with oil in the quiet bedroom, and have rejoiced in healing as a result of their obedience. Again there are the many prayer circles where written requests for healing are remembered before the Throne. The source of all healing virtue is in the Lord Jesus Christ, and although methods differ, the all-important matter is to get the sick into touch with Him.

DIVINE HEALING *V.* FAITH HEALING.

In studying bodily healing there are a few things that must be kept in mind. The first is the difference that can exist between Divine healing and what is known as faith healing. We prefer the former term because it generally implies belief in bodily healing as it is exclusively taught in the Scriptures, whereas the latter might mean healing by faith along the many lines of psychology. The former denotes acceptance of the Bible as the Word of God in its entirety, and healing through the Lord Jesus Christ. The latter can imply belief in any kind of faith healing that might be taught in books that are decidedly anti-Christian.

HEALING IN TWO REALMS: THE NATURAL.

The next thing to bear in mind is that healing can be obtained in two realms, namely, natural and supernatural. That healing comes along natural lines is clear to all. It has pleased God to manifest this in the animal creation as well as in the human creation. The beast of the field is healed of its wounds as a result of a natural law which operates, and it is the bounden duty of both saint and sinner to assist that law in every legitimate way. The suffering animal calls for due and proper attention, the withholding of which under any pretext would be cruel and inhuman. Who could conscientiously justify himself if, knowing any creature to be in pain, he did not, whenever possible, call in someone with ability to alleviate its suffering? The service of those who are qualified to co-ordinate with this natural law, in the suffering animal creation, can never be repaid; and the knowledge they possess should be counted among the many natural gifts bestowed by God upon His creation. At the same time supernatural healing in the animal world should not be ruled out, as most devoted saints have given indisputable testimonies to such healings. No less a person than John Wesley, the founder of Methodism, who was a firm believer in Divine healing, testifies in his journal to the remarkable deliverance of his faithful horse. We have known cases where God in answer to prayer has healed the cattle of saintly farmers who have claimed the promise in the seventh chapter of Deuteronomy, believing it to be one of those which are " yea and amen " in Christ.

> Wherefore it shall come to pass, if ye hearken to these judgments, and keep and do them, that the Lord thy God shall keep unto thee the covenant and the mercy which He sware unto thy fathers.
> And He will love thee, and bless thee, and multiply thee : He will also bless . . . the increase of thy kine, and the flocks of thy sheep, in the land which He sware unto thy fathers to give thee.
> And the Lord will take away from thee all sickness.—Deut. vii. 12, 13, 15.

When we come to consider the human creation, we find that God in His love and mercy has provided the means of healing for all mankind, saints and sinners alike, by the operation of a natural law which is inherent in the human organism. Physicians and nurses through much study have become acquainted with this natural law of healing ; consequently they can intelligently assist nature to heal or re-assert itself. They minister in the realm of the natural, and it is the duty and privilege of every Christian to pray for them in their work. We have come into contact with many who belong to the noble medical profession, and have never met one who claimed to have power to heal. The most they have asserted is that they possess the intelligence which enables them to assist nature to heal itself. An eminent physician clearly shewed the true position when on one occasion, after being complimented for his skill, he said, "I dressed the wound, and God healed it." Doctors and nurses only dispense the blessings which God has vouchsafed to mankind—just like those people who, irrespective of their standing before God, are used to dispense other blessings, such as the means of sustenance among the sons of men. How inconsistent a Christian would be if he spent much time in prayer for a good harvest and did not take time to plough the field, sow the seed, water the ground, and assist in every legitimate way the answer to his prayers. The natural law of healing, like sunshine and rain, is another of the manifold gifts that are bestowed through the goodness of God upon godly and ungodly alike, in order to lead men to repentance.

He maketh His sun to rise on the evil and on the good, and sendeth rain on the just and on the unjust.—Matt. v. 45.

Or despisest thou the riches of His goodness and forbearance and long-suffering; not knowing that the goodness of God leadeth thee to repentance.—Rom. ii. 4.

It is a huge mistake on the part of many devout believers in the truth of Divine Healing to ignore natural healing. Some earnest saints have regarded the work of physicians and nurses who minister in the natural realm as being distinctly evil or carnal. A few have gone so far as to disregard the essential laws of hygiene, to ignore natural curative means, and even refuse the absolute necessities of the body, in case they should manifest unbelief and dishonour God. Such indiscretion has hindered many from taking a stand for the truth, and often resulted in the work of God being brought into disrepute. It is most necessary that the truth of bodily healing should be viewed from the right perspective, and that its presentation be sane, sound, and balanced.

> Let not then your good be evil spoken of.—Rom. xiv. 16.

HEALING IN TWO REALMS: THE SUPERNATURAL.

Bodily healing in the supernatural realm is clearly taught throughout the whole range of Scripture. The Christian Church right down through the centuries has emphasised the truth that the Bible is the Word of God, that its commandments should be implicitly obeyed, and its promises believingly appropriated. Why then should it be a cause for wonderment if thousands, having believed its teaching, can testify to miracles and healings? Cases that are incurable in the natural realm have been healed in the supernatural. The Gospel narrative of the woman with the issue of blood reveals that she was beyond the aid of physicians. She had persistently sought healing along natural lines, even to the extent of spending all her living in vain. After much disappointment she summoned every effort, overcame every difficulty, gathered all remaining strength, made contact with a Physician of a higher realm, and was made perfectly whole.

> And a woman having an issue of blood twelve years, which had spent all her living upon physicians, neither could be healed of any,
> Came behind Him, and touched the border of His garment: and immediately her issue of blood stanched.—Luke viii. 43, 44.

HIGHER AND LOWER CRITICS.

Those who claim to believe in the miraculous in our day are confronted with two kinds of critics, the higher and the other, which we feel justified in designating the lower.

The higher critic is one who from an intellectual standpoint rejects the working of miracles—the highbrow who maintains the right to pick and choose the portions in the Bible which in his judgment are inspired. He

7

does not allow his mind to accept anything that cannot be explained within the range of reason. The lower critic is the one who unreservedly accepts the Bible as the inspired Word of God, but who endeavours to shew from its pages that we are not living in the days of miracles. If he cannot succeed in proving that the miraculous was withdrawn at the end of the apostolic days, he attempts to postpone the supernatural element to a future millennium. Of the two kinds of critics we must confess that the higher is far more consistent than the lower. The former commences by making it perfectly clear that while he believes the Bible contains the Word of God, he does not believe the whole Bible to be inspired. Therefore he is not inconsistent with the stand he takes when eliminating the miraculous from the Bible. Let us say though, in passing, that if he professes to be a minister of the Gospel, he is most inconsistent with his calling in denying the inspiration of any part of the Book. But the lower critic is most inconsistent with his own standpoint, and indeed presents a pitiable sight. He starts off by declaring his absolute faith in a present-day miraculous Bible with all its commands and its promises, and then argues that miracles are not for the present. His unreasonable attitude often proves the saying attributed to Spurgeon to be only too true— " The Gospel suffers more from its exponents than its opponents." How one can claim to

be evangelical and fundamental, and at the same
time deny the miraculous, is more than puzzling
to us. While professing to believe in a supernatural religion, he is all the time undermining
its foundation.

Why ! belief in the great truths of the new
birth and the second advent of Christ, which
most Christians hold, virtually implies belief in
the supernatural. It is impossible to account
for the experience of regeneration apart from
a miracle. This was the first lesson that
Nicodemus had to learn from the Master Himself. In response to his question, " How can
a man be born when he is old? " our Lord
gave him that all-important object lesson of the
wind. What is it that happens at regeneration?
The sinner receives pardon for all his sins, he
is definitely justified, and God commences to
deal with him as though he had never sinned.
The Spirit of Christ comes into his heart crying, " Abba, Father," and the regenerated one
is a partaker of the Creator's nature. Divine
nature is here blended with that of the sons of
men—a mystery of mysteries, the creation of
the Holy Ghost. How useless it is to try to
account for the new birth apart from the supernatural. Then again, what a glorious hope the
second advent of Christ is ! Christians everywhere are longing for His return. We maintain that to believe in the second advent of
Christ, and all that it entails, means believing

9

in a tremendous demonstration with supernatural effects.

> For the Lord Himself shall des-
> cend from heaven with a shout, with
> the voice of the archangel, and with
> the trump of God : and the dead in
> Christ shall rise first :
> Then we which are alive and re-
> main shall be caught up together
> with them in the clouds, to meet the
> Lord in the air : and so shall we ever
> be with the Lord.—I. Thess. iv.
> 16, 17.

At a certain convention we were privileged
to listen to a great student of Second Advent
truth preaching on his favourite theme. In his
address he graphically described the resurrection
of the dead saints, the translation of living
saints, the broken law of gravitation, and many
other remarkable happenings at the coming of
Christ. Some time afterwards we had occasion
to compare notes, and in the midst of our con-
versation he most emphatically declared that
the days of miracles were past. "This," he
said, "is an age of faith, without signs of any
kind." It is unnecessary to say that we re-
minded him of the teaching he had given in
his address, and how faithfully yet unknowingly
he declared that he believed in miracles in this
age. The second coming of Christ is to be the
closing act in the great dispensation of the Holy
Ghost. His coming will bring to a conclusion
the most miraculous dispensation in the whole
of God's dealings with mankind.

CHAPTER II

Some Effects of the First Adam's Disobedience

The first man Adam was made a living soul—
I. Cor. xv. 45.

The first man is of the earth earthy.—I. Cor. xv. 47.
For as by one man's disobedience . . .—Rom. v. 19.

IN order to get the right perspective for the teaching of scriptural healing it would be well for us to consider the indisputable teaching of Scripture concerning the original condition of man, the fall of Adam, and its effects upon mankind and creation ; also concerning the Saviour of mankind and the restoration of creation.

THE ORIGINAL CONDITION OF MAN, THE FIRST ADAM,

Adam, endued with splendid intellectual powers, was created in the image and likeness of God. He was invested with power and authority in three realms, on earth, on the sea, and in the air. He lived in a creation of exceeding beauty, and communed with his Creator in a state of absolute innocency. God's testimony to the work of His own hands is declared in the following verse :

God saw everything that He had made, and, behold, it was very good.
—Gen. i. 31.

11

THE FALL OF MAN AND ITS EFFECT UPON CREATION.

Adam, tempted by the Devil, fell by transgression from that state of innocency, and the whole creation, including the human family, the animal world, and the material earth, has suffered in consequence of that fall, according to the following scripture :

> For we know that the whole creation groaneth and travaileth in pain together until now.—Rom. viii. 22.

THE SAVIOUR OF MANKIND AND THE RESTORATION OF CREATION.

The Saviour of fallen humanity is the Lord Jesus Christ, the second Person in the Trinity, who, clothed with human nature, came into this world to destroy the works of the Devil, to save mankind by His atoning death on the cross, and to make it possible for the suffering creation to be delivered, according to the following scriptures :

> Forasmuch then as the children are partakers of flesh and blood, He also Himself likewise took part of the same ; that through death He might destroy him that had the power of death, that is, the devil.—Heb. ii. 14.
>
> Once in the end of the world hath He appeared to put away sin by the sacrifice of Himself.—Heb. ix. 26.
>
> For this purpose the Son of God

was manifested, that He might destroy the works of the devil.—I. John
iii. 8.

And He that sat upon the throne
said, Behold, I make all things new
. . .—Rev. xxi. 5.

Let us now tabulate some of the definite
results of the first Adam's disobedience, and
then consider some of the benefits of the last
Adam's obedience upon the whole of creation.

SIN.

" All have sinned." In these words the
Bible confirms the total moral depravity of the
human race. Scripture likens all to sheep that
have gone astray. It includes all under con-
demnation. It charges all with transgression
and makes no difference, for all have sinned.
Only one Man ever trod this earth who could
rightly claim to be the exception, and he was
the Man Christ Jesus, for He " knew no sin,
neither was guile found in His mouth." Amid
the wreck of fallen humanity He stands out as
the only One who actually condemned sin in
the flesh, and by virtue of His triumph He is
the able Saviour of mankind.

The condition of all others is most truthfully
and accurately depicted in the following
scriptures.

The Lord looked down from heaven
upon the children of men, to see if
there were any that did understand,
and seek God.

They are all gone aside, they are altogether become filthy: there is none that doeth good, no not one.—Psalm xiv. 2, 3.

All we like sheep have gone astray; we have turned every one to his own way; and the Lord hath laid on Him the iniquity of us all.—Isaiah liii. 6.

If Thou, Lord, shouldest mark iniquities, O Lord, who shall stand? —Psalm cxxx. 3.

As it is written, There is none righteous, no, not one.—Rom. iii. 10.

For all have sinned, and come short of the glory of God.—Rom. iii. 23,

DEATH.

"Death by sin." In just these few words the inspired Apostle explains the advent of this last enemy of mankind. Before sin there were no death, no heartbreakings, no separation from loved ones, no funeral processions, no graveyards. Now graves are opened, there are sorrowing ones, and acute separations from those loved most. The hands that once ministered to the needy are helpless, the eyes that pitied the less fortunate are glazed, the feet that went on errands of mercy walk that way no more, the tongue of the eloquent is stilled in silence, the heart of the compassionate ceases to beat; all faculties fail, and the body, that organism so fearfully and wonderfully made, is laid to rest amidst the ashes of earth. Legislators have made laws with fearful penalties, orators have delivered eloquent lectures on the maintenance of health, and scientists have put forth superhuman efforts in the struggle of life, all with a view to postponing the operation of death. Still it rages with a fearful fury, and reigns in every nation from the northern to the southern poles, from the eastern to the western shores. It affects alike the monarch and the subject, the peer and the pauper, the learned and the unlearned, the high and the low, the rich and the poor, in every country under the canopy of heaven.

> Wherefore, as by one man sin entered into the world, and death by sin; and so death passed upon all men, for that all have sinned.—Rom. v. 12.
>
> The last enemy that shall be destroyed is death.—I. Cor. xv. 26.

THE ANIMAL KINGDOM IN BONDAGE.

Most people overlook the fact that the animal kingdom is suffering in bondage as a result of the first Adam's transgression. Yet this is clearly taught in the Word of God. All are prepared to admit that there is much suffering among animals, for it is impossible to live in this world without coming into contact with it, sometimes in the most acute form. The sensibilities of even the unemotional are at times wounded by the reports of cases which are brought before magistrates for cruelty to animals. The bondage of corruption, with all the suffering and pain that emanate from it, is the direct result of the Fall. Creatures that were once docile and harmless suddenly became wild and ferocious. Who could possibly imagine beasts with savage and cruel instincts roaming about within the confines of a blessed and tranquil Eden? The animal creation fell when Adam fell, and ever since the groanings of burdened creatures have fallen upon the most insensitive ears.

Before the Fall Adam had dominion over everything that moved upon the earth, and it was not until he departed from his allegiance to his Maker that the animal creation became involved.

> For the creature was made subject to vanity, not willingly, but by reason of Him who hath subjected the same in hope,
> Because the creature itself also shall be delivered from the bondage of corruption into the glorious liberty of the children of God.—Rom. viii. 20, 21.

THE CURSE UPON THE EARTH.

Thorns and thistles bear witness to the curse that came upon the earth as a result of the first Adam's disobedience. Through sin the ground which brought forth plentifully, tender grass and herb yielding seed after its kind, and trees laden with luscious fruits, came under the bondage of corruption, and the earth, which

16

was to produce the means of sustenance for a never-ending life, suddenly became necessary as a burial place for the dead. As a result of the curse mother earth is in bondage, and the vegetable kingdom labours increasingly to bring forth. This possibly explains why the writer of the Epistle to the Hebrews declared that the earth would wax old as doth a garment. To meet the present needs mankind has to resort to using chemicals for the purpose of forcing production. The mighty energies of nature are being held in check, and the earth, labouring under the curse, cannot possibly produce as it could in the Eden state. The sweat that breaks out on the husbandman's brow as he tills the land, and the sorrow with which he eats of its produce, bear witness with the thorn and the thistle to the perpetuity of the curse.

> . . . Cursed is the ground for thy sake; in sorrow shalt thou eat of it all the days of thy life;
>
> Thorns also and thistles shall it bring forth to thee; and thou shalt eat the herb of the field;
>
> In the sweat of thy face shalt thou eat bread, till thou return unto the ground; for out of it wast thou taken: for dust thou art, and unto dust shalt thou return.—Gen. iii. 17, 18, 19.

MORTALITY.

Mortality, which means " subject to death," is the portion of sinner and believer alike, right from the womb to the grave. It is a term that belongs to the living, and not to the unborn or dead. There is a beginning and end in mortality, proved beyond the shadow of doubt by the span of life that is allotted to mankind in general. Mortality confirms the teaching of Scripture concerning fallen human nature, or, in other words, physical depravity. The fact that no member of the human family, whether saint or sinner, is immune from sickness, disease, and decay, proves that all suffer from the limitations of fallen human nature. It is one of the results of the first Adam's disobedience, one of the many that quickly followed in the trail of sin. The believer delivered from the chains of sin—moral depravity— through the blood of Christ, still has to contend with the weaknesses of physical depravity. He is confined to a body which groans, earnestly desiring for the day to come when mortality shall be swallowed up of life.

> Nevertheless death reigned from Adam to Moses, even over them that had not sinned after the similitude of Adam's transgression, who is the figure of Him that was to come.— Rom. v. 14.
>
> Because the creature itself also shall be delivered from the bondage of corruption into the glorious liberty of the children of God.
>
> For we know that the whole creation groaneth and travaileth in pain together until now.

> And not only they, but ourselves also, which have the firstfruits of the Spirit, even we ourselves groan within ourselves, waiting for the adoption, to wit, the redemption of our body.
> —Rom. viii. 21, 22, 23.

SICKNESS AND DISEASE.

Although there is no definite scripture to shew that sickness and disease came into this world as a result of the first Adam's disobedience, it is only reasonable to deduce this from certain scriptures which we shall consider in our fourth chapter.

Before sin there was no death ; and if there was no death, there was no physical depravity ; and if there was no physical depravity, there could have been no sickness and disease. The breaking of God's moral law entails suffering from such diseases as are catalogued in the twenty-eighth chapter of Deuteronomy. The world suffering from the effects of the Fall has become the stage for a drama of woe. The smitten, the bound, the oppressed, the bruised, the broken, the maimed, the lame, the blind, the dumb, the deaf, all in a seeming endless procession play their part, and pass on to the accompaniment of the dirge of sighs and groans of distress. From the dust of each succeeding generation arises another to carry on and suffer. The wail of anguish is not stifled in the throes of death before it is heard re-echoing along the ranks of those who follow in their trail. The scenery behind the moving mass of frail humanity depicts the prison, the hospital, the asylum, the charnel house, and the graveyard. Here we have the wan cheek, the imbecile child, the languid look, the lustreless eye, the frail frame, the infant feebleness, the preying plague, and the devouring cancer. Waves of sorrow as mountains high pass over the earth with its expansive seas of sickness, and its battlefields sodden with the blood of youth. Violence and cruelty, murder, and oppression stalk through the land amidst the bruised and the broken, until the whole world seems sick and ready to die.

> Wherefore, as by one man sin entered into the world, and death by sin; and so death passed upon all men, for that all have sinned.—Rom. v. 12.
>
> Fools because of their transgression, and because of their iniquities, are afflicted.—Psalm cvii. 17.

CHAPTER III

Some of the Benefits of the Last Adam's Obedience

The last Adam was made a quickening Spirit.—
I. Cor. xv. 45.

*The Lord from heaven.—*I. Cor. xv. 47.

*Became obedient unto death.—*Phil. ii. 8.

IN the last chapter we briefly looked at the teaching of Scripture concerning—

1. The original condition of the first man, Adam, and the world in which he lived.

2. The fall of that man and its disastrous effects upon the whole world.

3. The coming of Christ into this fallen world as Saviour and Deliverer.

We then considered in more detail the teaching of Scripture concerning some of the effects of the fall which were as follows—

1. Sin.
2. Death.
3. The bondage of the animal kingdom.
4. The curse upon the earth.
5. Mortality.
6. Sickness and disease.

21

We have now arrived at the juncture when two questions will naturally arise.

Firstly. Does the atoning and redeeming work of Christ upon the cross make provision for putting away sin with all its evil effects?

Secondly. If it does, can we claim the full benefits of the atoning and redeeming work in the present?

The answer to the first is in the affirmative, for Scripture certainly teaches the following :

(a) That Christ came into the world to put away sin through His atoning death on the cross.

> Nor yet that He should offer Himself often, as the high priest entereth into the holy place every year with blood of others ;
> For then must He often have suffered since the foundation of the world : but now once in the end of the world hath He appeared *to put away sin* by the sacrifice of Himself.
> —Heb. ix. 25, 26.

(b) That sin with all its effects which are the works of the Devil who instigated the Fall are to be destroyed.

> He that committeth sin is of the devil; for the devil sinneth from the beginning. For this purpose the Son of God was manifested, that He might destroy the works of the devil.—
> I. John iii. 8.

(c) That the whole creation is to be completely delivered from the bondage of corruption to which it is now subjected.

> And He that sat upon the throne said, Behold, I make all things new. And He said unto me, Write: for these words are true and faithful.— Rev. xxi. 5.

If sin, the cause of all the evil effects from which the creation is suffering, could only be put away by the atoning work of Christ upon the cross, then it is only reasonable to conclude that provision has been made in that atoning and redeeming work for the putting away of its effects.

We shall now consider the deliverance from each of the separate effects of the first Adam's disobedience that we have enumerated, in order to give the correct answer to the second question, namely, Can we claim the full benefits of the atoning and redeeming work of Christ in the present?

DELIVERANCE FROM SIN—A PRESENT-DAY EXPERIENCE.

Deliverance from the penalty and power of sin through the blood of Christ is most assuredly taught throughout the Bible. The atonement of Christ has been and always will be the sovereign remedy for sin. Multitudes have experienced its cleansing power and have confirmed the Scripture testimony that the

Blood cleanses from all sin. It is clearly taught as a present-day experience for all who believe and it is not necessary to wait for a future dispensation to know the cleansing efficacy of the precious Blood. It was the experience of righteous Abel when he offered the more excellent sacrifice which typified Christ the Lamb of God, who would lay down His life upon the cross that loomed in the distance. The atoning work of Christ was the rock upon which father Abraham built when belief was counted unto him for righteousness. It was the theme of the long line of saintly prophets and noble patriarchs in the Old Testament, for they were forgiven and saved by the Blood which their sacrifices foreshadowed. New Testament saints all join together in one chorus of praise for the Blood that has cleansed them. The main theme of Christian apostles, prophets, teachers, pastors, evangelists throughout all time is salvation from the penalty and power of sin through Christ. Forgiveness, pardon, cleansing are words that certainly belong to the vernacular of those who have been saved through the blood of the Lamb.

But if we walk in the light, as He is in the light, we have fellowship one with another, and the blood of Jesus Christ His Son cleanseth us from all sin.—I. John i. 7.

Who His own self bare our sins in His own body on the tree, that we being dead to sins, should live unto righteousness: by whose stripes ye were healed.—I. Peter ii. 24.

Be it known unto you therefore, men and brethren, that through this Man is preached unto you the forgiveness of sins.—Acts xiii. 38.

Now when they heard this, they were pricked in their heart, and said unto Peter and to the rest of the apostles, Men and brethren; what shall we do?

Then Peter said unto them, Repent, and be baptised every one of you in the Name of Jesus Christ for the remission of sins, and ye shall receive the gift of the Holy Ghost.—Acts ii. 37, 38.

DELIVERANCE FROM DEATH RESERVED FOR THE FUTURE.

God can grant immunity from death and He can cause the dead to be raised by His power in our day, for He is omnipotent. But it would be wrong for anyone to teach victory over death on the assumption that He can and may grant it in the present dispensation. We can only teach with certainty deliverance from the things which He has definitely promised in His Word. Immunity from death is reserved for the day when mortals shall put on immortality at the coming of Christ and when the dead in Christ shall be raised incorruptible. To preach deliverance from death in the present dispensation of grace, before the

25

coming of Christ, would certainly mean going beyond scriptural authority. Even in the miraculous signs that were promised by Christ in confirmation of the preached Word when He commissioned the disciples to go and preach the Gospel throughout the world and to every creature, it is conspicuous by its absence. Although death itself will not be destroyed until the future, the believer in Christ can be delivered from the fear of death in the present. Through Christ immunity from the fear of death can be his happy experience, and when called upon to pass over from the scene of time into the presence of the Lord he can just fall asleep in the Everlasting Arms.

Forasmuch then as the children are partakers of flesh and blood, He also Himself likewise took part of the same; that through death He might destroy him that had the power of death, that is, the devil.

And deliver them who through fear of death were all their lifetime subject to bondage.—Heb. ii. 14, 15.

For this corruptible must put on incorruption, and this mortal must put on immortality.

So when this corruptible shall have put on incorruption, and this mortal shall have put on immortality, then shall be brought to pass the saying that is written, Death is swallowed up in victory.

26

O death, where is thy sting? O
grave, where is thy victory?—I. Cor.
xv. 53-55.

DELIVERANCE OF THE ANIMAL KINGDOM RESERVED FOR THE FUTURE.

Yes, the groanings of this burdened creation
are to cease, the poignantly pathetic sufferings
of the dumb are to pass away for ever and the
animal creation is to merge suddenly into a
state of blessedness, all as a result of the last
Adam's obedience. The wild ferocious
members of the lower creation with their
savage and cruel instincts are to become new
creatures indeed. The effect of the atoning
and redeeming work of Christ upon the cross
is going to be seen in the new creation that
shall rise out of the bondage of corruption. In
the present we have to content ourselves with
doing all that is in our power to alleviate the
sufferings of the burdened creation and pray on
behalf of the activities of all men and women
who so nobly band themselves under various
banners for the protection of the dumb and
suffering. In millennial times the beasts of the
earth instead of preying upon and devouring
one another will enter into a new relationship :
the wolf and the lamb shall feed together, the
leopard shall lie down with the kid, the calf and
the young lion shall be together ; for, saith the
Lord, '' they shall not hurt nor destroy in all
My holy mountain.'' Prophecies relating to
the deliverance of the animal creation from the

bondage of corruption will be fulfilled, the moment that Jesus, who paid the price for its emancipation, takes His place on the throne of David.

> Because the creature itself also shall be delivered from the bondage of corruption into the glorious liberty of the children of God.—Rom. viii. 21.
>
> And righteousness shall be the girdle of His loins, and faithfulness the girdle of His reins.
>
> The wolf also shall dwell with the lamb, and the leopard shall lie down with the kid; and the calf and the young lion and the fatling together; and a little child shall lead them.
>
> And the cow and the bear shall feed; their young ones shall lie down together: and the lion shall eat straw like the ox.
>
> And the sucking child shall play on the hole of the asp, and the weaned child shall put his hand on the cockatrice' den.
>
> They shall not hurt nor destroy in all My holy mountain: for the earth shall be full of the knowledge of the Lord, as the waters cover the sea. —Isaiah xi. 5-9.

REMOVAL OF THE CURSE FROM THE EARTH RESERVED FOR THE FUTURE.

The removal of the curse that at present rests upon mother earth, as a result of the first Adam's disobedience, is a certainty of the future. Then the mighty energies of nature which are now held in check will break forth and the ground will become so fertile that it shall produce superabundantly. The earth, which in our day has waxed old like a well-worn garment, will be renewed, and the glowing description of its fertility given in psalm and prophecy be realised. Toil will become a pleasure ; poverty and want shall be unknown ; for the ploughman shall overtake the reaper, and there will be enough and to spare. The curse will have been removed as a result of the atoning and redeeming work of Christ on the cross. The benefits of the last Adam's obedience will be seen in the changed condition of the earth during millennial days. We have known special blessing to rest upon lands of Christian farmers in answer to prayer in the present age, but the full deliverance from the curse will not take place until Christ takes the throne.

> And they shall build houses and inhabit them; and they shall plant vineyards, and eat the fruit of them.
>
> They shall not build, and another inhabit; they shall not plant, and another eat : for as the days of a tree are the days of My people, and Mine elect shall long enjoy the work of their hands.—Isaiah lxv. 21, 22.
>
> Behold, the days come, saith the Lord, that the plowman shall overtake the reaper, and the treader of grapes him that soweth seed; and the mountains shall drop sweet wine, and all the hills shall melt.

> And I will bring again the captivity
> of My people of Israel, and they shall
> build the waste cities, and inhabit
> them; and they shall plant vineyards,
> and drink the wine thereof; they shall
> also make gardens, and eat the fruit
> of them.—Amos ix. 13, 14.

DELIVERANCE FROM MORTALITY—WHEN CHRIST COMES.

Immortality is not promised to mankind in the present dispensation. God can bestow immortality upon believers in this age, and can translate them to heaven as He did Enoch and Elijah, for He is omnipotent. But we are not justified in teaching saints to claim such an experience in the present age on the ground of our Lord's omnipotence. We can rightly teach believers to claim experiences which are definitely promised in the Word of God, but immortality is not promised to anyone before the second advent of Christ. It is reserved until the moment of His arrival in the air, when all living born-again believers will be taken up to meet Him. Until then all believers can rejoice in the hope, while patiently waiting within the bounds of mortality for that glorious moment. In the present dispensation believers are in the waiting room, subject it is true to the limitation of the mortal body. Saints and sinners alike grow old, the eye becomes dim, the back bent, and the effects of mortality, which does not necessarily mean sickness and disease, are marked upon all, even those who take a stand for the truth of Divine healing. Nevertheless, how consoling it is to know that the bodies of believers are the present dwelling place of God. They were included in the great purchase price, not that of corruptible silver and gold, but the precious blood of Christ. Thus the benefits of His atoning and redeeming work will be seen in the complete redemption of the mortal body.

> And not only they, but ourselves also, which have the firstfruits of the Spirit, even we ourselves groan within ourselves, waiting for the adoption, to wit, the redemption of our body. —Rom. viii. 23.
>
> Behold, I shew you a mystery; We shall not all sleep, but we shall all be changed,
>
> In a moment, in the twinkling of an eye, at the last trump: for the trumpet shall sound, and the dead shall be raised incorruptible, and we shall be changed.
>
> For this corruptible must put on incorruption, and this mortal must put on immortality.
>
> So when this corruptible shall have put on incorruption, and this mortal shall have put on immortality, then shall be brought to pass the saying that is written, Death is swallowed up in victory.
>
> O death, where is thy sting? O grave, where is thy victory?—I. Cor. xv. 51-55.
>
> For our conversation is in heaven:

31

from whence also we look for the Saviour, the Lord Jesus Christ:

Who shall change this body of our humiliation that it may be fashioned like unto the body of His glory.—Phil. iii. 20, 21.

BODILY HEALING FROM SICKNESS AND DISEASE A PRESENT-DAY EXPERIENCE.

Scripture abounds in testimonies of those who have enjoyed the immediate benefits of bodily healing. Abimelech, his wife, and his maid-servants were healed in answer to the prayer of Abraham. Miriam was healed of leprosy in answer to the prayer of Moses. King Hezekiah was healed, and had his life prolonged fifteen years. The woman who suffered twelve years with the issue of blood was healed when she touched her Lord. The lame man at the gate of the Temple was healed when Peter commanded him to rise in the Name of Jesus of Nazareth. Our Lord distinctly included bodily healing as an immediate benefit among the miraculous signs that were to follow them that believe. Saints throughout the centuries have since testified to bodily healing—see chapters ix., x., and xii.

And He said unto them, Go ye into all the world, and preach the Gospel to every creature . . .

They shall take up serpents; and if they drink any deadly thing, it shall not hurt them; they shall lay hands on the sick, and they shall recover. —Mark xvi. 15, 18.

Is any sick among you? let him call for the elders of the church; and let them pray over him, anointing him with oil in the Name of the Lord:

And the prayer of faith shall save the sick, and the Lord shall raise him up; and if he have committed sins, they shall be forgiven him.— James v. 14, 15.

The following chart will briefly summarise our studies up to this point.

<table>
<tr><td colspan="2">Original Condition and Results of First Adam's Disobedience as described in the Word of God.</td><td colspan="2">Present and Ultimate Benefits of Last Adam's Obedience definitely promised in the Word of God.</td></tr>
</table>

Original condition.	Present condition confirmed by experience.	Present benefits confirmed by experience.	Future benefits.
No sin.	Sin.	Deliverance from sin.	
No death.	Death.	—	Death destroyed.
No bondage in the animal kingdom.	Bondage in the animal kingdom.	—	Animals delivered.
No curse on the earth.	Curse resting on the earth.	—	Curse removed.
No mortality.	Mortality.	—	Immortality.
No bodily sickness.	Bodily sickness.	Bodily healing.	

Healing Rays

The atoning and redeeming work of Christ on the cross is the sovereign remedy for all the evil results of the first Adam's disobedience. The future benefits of the last Adam's death on the cross include the destruction of the last enemy, which is death, the deliverance of the animal kingdom from the bondage of corruption, the removal of the curse that rests upon the earth, and the superseding of mortality by immortality. The present benefits of His atoning and redeeming work include deliverance from sin and healing for the mortal body. Before Calvary saints of God looked forward to the Cross, and claimed in their day the benefits of salvation and healing. Saints after Calvary look backward to the Cross, and claim the present benefits of salvation and healing. Saints of all ages will ultimately participate in the joy of seeing every evil effect of the first Adam's disobedience completely done away with, all because the last Adam became obedient unto death, even the death of the Cross.

But made Himself of no reputation, and took upon Him the form of a servant, and was made in the likeness of men;

And being found in fashion as a man, He humbled Himself, and became obedient unto death, even the death of the cross.—Phil. ii. 7, 8.

In whom we have redemption through His blood, the forgiveness of sins, according to the riches of His grace;

Wherein He hath abounded toward us in all wisdom and prudence;

Having made known unto us the mystery of His will, according to His good pleasure which He hath purposed in Himself:

That in the dispensation of the fulness of times He might gather together in one all things in Christ, both which are in heaven, and which are on earth; even in Him.—Eph. i. 7-10.

The eyes of your understanding being enlightened; that ye may know what is the hope of His calling, and what the riches of the glory of His inheritance in the saints,

And what is the exceeding greatness of His power to usward who believe, according to the working of His mighty power,

Which He wrought in Christ, when He raised Him from the dead, and set Him at His own right hand in the heavenly places,

Far above all principality, and power, and might, and dominion, and every name that is named, not only in this world, but also in that which is to come:

And hath put all things under His feet, and gave Him to be head over all things to the church,

Which is His body, the fulness of Him that filleth all in all.—Eph. i. 18-23.

Healing Rays

What shall we then say to these things? If God be for us, who can be against us?

He that spared not His own Son, but delivered Him up for us all, how shall He not with Him also freely give us all things?—Rom. viii. 31, 32.

CHAPTER IV

The Source of Sickness and Disease

|Scriptural Affirmations—Logical Deductions

WE have now definitely established three main lines of scriptural teaching.

Firstly, that sin, sickness, death, mortality, the curse upon the earth and the bondage of corruption from which the animal creation suffers came into this world as a result of the first Adam's disobedience.

Secondly, that the atoning and redeeming work of Christ on the cross is the sovereign remedy for all the evil effects of the first Adam's disobedience.

Thirdly, that while we can claim deliverance from part of these effects in the present, we have to wait until some future time before the full benefits of the atoning and redeeming work of Christ on the cross can be realised.

There are some facts that should be remembered when we come to seek information regarding the source of sickness and disease :

Firstly. There must have been a beginning to sickness and disease just as there was a beginning to sin.

37

Secondly. There is no scripture to shew that sickness and disease can be traced back to God. Indeed it would be almost sacrilege to conceive of such a possibility.

Thirdly. There is no definite scripture to shew that sickness and disease can be traced back to Satan.

One question will now naturally arise. Does Scripture throw any light upon this important point? Yes! the light comes after a little careful consideration of the following facts which are based upon Scripture.

Firstly. That Scripture definitely shews that *sin* can be traced back to its source, which is Satan.

> He that committeth sin is of the devil; for the devil sinneth from the beginning.—I. John iii. 8.
> Ye are of your father the devil, and the lusts of your father ye will do. He was a murderer from the beginning, and abode not in the truth, because there is no truth in him. When he speaketh a lie, he speaketh of his own: for he is a liar and the father of it.—John viii. 44.

Secondly. That Scripture definitely shews that death can be traced back to sin.

> Wherefore, as by one man sin entered into the world, and death by sin; and so death passed upon all men, for that all have sinned.—Rom. v. 12.

The Source of Sickness and Disease

With these things clearly stated before us, it will not be difficult to come to a fairly safe conclusion as regards the source of all sickness and disease. If death can be definitely traced back to sin, and if sin can be definitely traced back to Satan and no further, we are not violating the principles of reasonable deduction when we maintain that sickness and disease, the harbingers of death, which are the processes leading to death, come from the same source. The Bible reveals Satan as a personal Devil, who is opposed to God and the human race. One who has power over sinners and who wages a real war against the saints. Amongst the many prevalent forms of unbelief in our day is the denial of the personality, and even the existence, of this awful being, designated, Satan.

Some people, though acknowledging his existence, have very little conception of his power and work among the children of men. No one is more pleased than Satan if he succeeds in getting men to regard him as the personification of sin and not the real Devil as revealed in Scripture. This mysterious being long before the days of Adam caused the ruin of the beautiful and perfect pre-Adamic creation of Genesis i. 1. In the beginning God created the heaven and the earth. This creation had its foundations laid amidst rejoicing, for the morning stars sang together and the sons of God shouted for joy. The changed condition of things, described in Genesis i. 2, as being void and without form, was brought about through the agency of Satan. Therefore we are not surprised to find him on earth after its reconstruction, and after man had been created in the image of God, instigating another dreadful fall. Satan was not always found in the form of a serpent as we see him in the Garden of Eden. He had occupied the highest place of honour among created beings, and had probably been nearest to the uncreated eternal Son of God. In the Garden of Eden he beguiles our first parents and leads them along the road of ambition, pride, and rebellion that had brought about his own downfall. Having obeyed his voice, the human family began its course of sorrow, suffering, and sickness in a world that has become a veritable valley of tears.

The following verses, concerning the works of the Devil, are from the pen of the Rev. A. J. Hough:

Men don't believe in a devil now, as their fathers
    used to do;
They've forced the door of the broadest creed to let
    his majesty through.
There isn't the print of his cloven foot or a fiery dart
    from his bow
To be found in earth or air to-day, for the world
    has voted so.

The Source of Sickness and Disease

But who is it mixing the fatal draught that palsies
  heart and brain,
And loads the bier of each passing year with ten
  hundred thousand slain?
Who blights the bloom of the land to-day with the
  fiery breath of hell,
If the devil isn't and never was? Won't somebody
  rise and tell?

Who dogs the steps of the toiling saint, and digs
  the pits for his feet?
Who sows the tares in the field of time wherever
  God sows His wheat?
The devil is voted not to be, and of course the thing
  is true;
But who is doing the kind of work the devil alone
  should do?

We are told he does not go about as a roaring lion
  now;
But whom shall we hold responsible for the everlasting row
To be heard in home, in church and state, to earth's
  remotest bound,
If the devil, by unanimous vote, is nowhere to be
  found?

Won't somebody step to the front forthwith, and
  make his bow, and shew
How the frauds and the crimes of a single day spring
  up? We want to know.
The devil was fairly voted out, and, of course, the
  devil's gone;
But simple folk would like to know who carries his
  business on?

Having traced sickness and disease to Satan
the arch-enemy of the human family, we will

now seek a Scriptural answer to the following question. Is Satan the only one who can afflict the sons of men with sickness and disease? The Bible clearly furnishes the following answers:

(1) That sickness can be inflicted by Satan upon saints and sinners alike under the permissive will of God.

> So went Satan forth from the presence of the Lord, and smote Job with sore boils from the sole of his foot unto his crown.
> And he took him a potsherd to scrape himself withal; and he sat down among the ashes.—Job ii. 7. 8.
> And ought not this woman, being a daughter of Abraham, whom Satan hath bound, lo, these eighteen years, be loosed from this bond on the sabbath day?—Luke xiii. 16.
> How God anointed Jesus of Nazareth with the Holy Ghost and with power: who went about doing good, and healing all that were oppressed of the devil; for God was with Him.
> —Acts x. 38.

(2) That saints and sinners alike can be afflicted with sickness by a direct act of God in the interests of justice or for the discipline of humanity.

> For the Lord will pass through to smite the Egyptians; and when He seeth the blood upon the lintel, and on the two sideposts, the Lord will

pass over the door, and will not suffer the destroyer to come in unto your houses to smite you.

And it came to pass, that at midnight the Lord smote all the firstborn in the land of Egypt, from the firstborn of Pharaoh that sat on his throne unto the firstborn of the captive that was in the dungeon, and all the firstborn of cattle.—Exod. xii. 23, 29.

And Jacob was left alone; and there wrestled a man with him until the breaking of the day.

And when he saw that he prevailed not against him, he touched the hollow of his thigh, and the hollow of Jacob's thigh was out of joint, as he wrestled with him.

And Jacob called the name of the place Peniel: for I have seen God face to face, and my life is preserved. —Gen. xxxii. 24, 25, 30.

And the angel answering said unto him, I am Gabriel, that stand in the presence of God, and am sent to speak unto thee, and to shew thee these glad tidings.

And, behold, thou shalt be dumb, and not able to speak, until the day that these things shall be performed, because thou believest not my words, which shall be fulfilled in their season.

And the people waited for Zacharias, and marvelled that he tarried so long in the temple.

And when he came out, he could not speak unto them: and they perceived that he had seen a vision in

the temple : for he beckoned unto
them and remained speechless.—
Luke i. 19-22.

Rev. T. De Witt Talmage, preaching from
Isa. vii. 20, said : " God is so kind and loving
that when it is necessary for Him to cut, He
has to go to others for the sharp-edged weapon.
' In the same day shall the Lord shave with
a razor that is hired, namely by them beyond
the river, by the King of Assyria, the head,
and the hair of the feet ; and it shall also con-
sume the beard.' God is love. God is pity.
God is help. God is shelter. God is rescue.
There are no sharp edges about Him, no
thrusting points, no instruments of laceration.
If you want balm for wounds, He has that.
If you want salve for Divine eyesight, He has
that. But if there is sharp and cutting work
to do which requires a razor, that He hires.
God has nothing about Him that hurts, save
when dire necessity demands ; and then He has
to go clear off to someone else to get the instrument.''

(3) That saints and sinners alike can be
afflicted with sickness and disease as a result
of breaking moral laws, natural laws, disre-
garding the laws of hygiene, and becoming
involved in all kinds of disasters and catas-
trophes to which this world is subject.

Fools because of their transgression, and because of their iniquities,
are afflicted.

> Their soul abhorreth all manner of meat; and they draw near unto the gates of death.—Psa. cvii. 17, 18.
>
> Be not deceived; God is not mocked: for whatsoever a man soweth, that shall he also reap.—Gal. vi. 7.
>
> Ye shall walk in all the ways which the Lord your God hath commanded you; that ye may live, and that it may be well with you, and that ye may prolong your days in the land which ye shall possess.—Deut. v. 33.

The difference between the saint and the sinner is that the former can pray and believe for the protection of his loving heavenly Father from some of the effects of the first Adam's disobedience, and from the disorders and calamities that are taking place in the world.

> Many are the afflictions of the righteous: but the Lord delivereth him out of them all.—Psa. xxxiv. 19.
>
> He that dwelleth in the secret place of the most High shall abide under the shadow of the Almighty.—Psa. xci. 1.

The sinner outside of the Divine will cannot expect to be protected, because he refuses to fall into line with the will of God. Yet in the sinner's case God lovingly lavishes blessings of all kinds upon him, ofttimes saving him from disasters, and even healing him of his diseases with a view to leading him to repentance.

Who will have all men to be saved, and to come unto the knowledge of the truth.—I. Tim. ii. 4.

And this is the confidence that we have in Him, that, if we ask any thing according to His will, He heareth us.—I. John v. 14.

Or despisest thou the riches of His goodness and forbearance and longsuffering; not knowing that the goodness of God leadeth thee to repentance?—Rom. ii. 4.

CHAPTER V

The Marvellous Mortal Body

1 will praise Thee, for I am fearfully and wonderfully made, marvellous are Thy works; and that my soul knoweth right well.—Psalm cxxxix. 14.

THE mortal body matters little : the salvation of the soul is far more important. It is selfish to be concerned about one's body : better give your whole time to the spiritual, for it is more glorifying to God. To be delivered from aches and pains is nothing to be compared with the deliverance from sin.

These and many other arguments are generally used by those who either oppose or neglect the teaching of bodily healing. We certainly agree that the spiritual is far more important than the physical, and salvation more than healing. Yet there is the possibility of one losing sight of the relationship between the spiritual and natural, and of underestimating the importance which the Scriptures give to the mortal body. It will not necessitate much discernment to perceive that objections framed in language of this kind come chiefly from the Lord's people, for their speech betrays them. They talk in the vernacular of the spiritual realm. Words such as ''salvation,'' ''spiritual,''

" deliverance," belong to the vocabulary of the redeemed. The terms " salvation of the soul " and " deliverance from sin " are such as are freely expressed by those who know Christ as Saviour. Thus it is the more astonishing to find Christians filling their mouths with arguments in order to disprove the clearly defined scriptural teaching of Divine Healing.

Our purpose in this chapter is to shew the importance that is attached to the mortal body in Scripture and to emphasise its relations to the different aspects of the Gospel message.

A MARVELLOUS ORGANISM.

" Fearfully and wonderfully made "—such was the conclusion of the Psalmist after meditating upon the astounding mechanism of the human frame. If he possessed the information given to us to-day by those who know, one can easily account for his ecstatic utterances. It has been estimated that there are some 725,000,000 air chambers in the lungs and that their total surface is about 2,000 square feet. Ten million nerves in one human body, thirty million pores in the body of a well-developed person, the heart beating 4,300 times an hour, throwing out $2\frac{1}{2}$ ozs. of blood at every pulsation, amounting to no less than 8 tons in a single day. The heart of one person who lives the allotted span of seventy years lifts no less than two hundred and seventy millions tons of blood.

The Marvellous Mortal Body

A person breathes 1,200 breaths an hour, inhaling thereby 600 gallons of air. Then think of the quickness of thought, the storehouse of memory, the secrets of the subconscious self, the wonderful eyeballs, the finger-prints, and the marvels of sight, hearing and feeling. If such calculation and description of the body that moves within the confines of mortality be correct, then what will it be like when mortality shall be swallowed up of life?

THE MORTAL BODY CHANGES MASTERS

Know ye not that to whom ye yield yourselves servants to obey, his servants ye are to whom ye obey; whether of sin unto death, or of obedience unto righteousness.

But God be thanked, that ye were the servants of sin, but ye have obeyed from the heart that form of doctrine which was delivered you.

Being then made free from sin, ye became the servants of righteousness.—Rom. vi. 16-18.

If this scripture means anything it is, that by the attitude of the body towards sin and righteousness, one can determine whether a person is saved or not. If he yields the members of his body to sin (by this of course is implied the continual yielding to sin as the habitual rule of life), then he is a servant of sin, and needs salvation. If he yields the

49

members of his body to righteousness (by this is implied obeying God as the habitual rule of life), then he is a servant of righteousness, and is a saved person. In each case the body, so to speak, is the indicator that reveals the actual condition of the person before God.

This being the case it is logical to conclude that a change takes place at conversion, not only as regards the soul and spirit, but the body too. In other words the deeds of the body are different after conversion from what they were before. We fail to find a single verse in the whole of the Bible to shew that salvation can be received by any person unless he is prepared to undergo such a change. Repentance towards God and faith in the Lord Jesus Christ are absolutely essential before any person can be saved. He must turn from the world, its folly, and its sin, to God, through the finished work of Christ upon the cross. He is then made what Paul calls a new creation, the things and deeds of the old life having passed away. The testimony of a really saved person is confirmed by the deeds of the body, which indicate the state of the soul.

The idea that eternal life is a gift that can be obtained by any sinner unconditionally, is as false and unscriptural as the notion that it can be merited by works. The forgiveness of past sins is only granted to those who by the grace of God decide not to continue in sin. How utterly helpless and hopeless any earthly government would be if it released all its prisoners and allowed them to continue as aforetime breaking the laws of the land. Civilisation, yea, the whole world, would soon be reduced to a state of irrevocable ruin. The sinner at conversion enters into a new life which reveals itself in the changed deeds of his body. Before conversion he is a drunkard, after conversion a sober man ; before conversion he is a thief, after conversion he is honest ; before conversion his lips blaspheme, after conversion they praise God. The change is at once admitted because his body acts differently. The body is the medium through which the new life is made manifest.

THE MORTAL BODY QUICKENED.

> But if the Spirit of Him that raised up Jesus from the dead dwell in you, He that raised up Christ from the dead shall also quicken your mortal bodies by His Spirit that dwelleth in you.—Rom. viii. 11.

Paul in his epistle to the Corinthian church declares that the mortal body has been purchased in addition to soul and spirit. There is no possibility of mistaking his message :

> What ! Know ye not that your body is the temple of the Holy Ghost which is in you, which ye have of God, and ye are not your own?

Healing Rays

> For ye are bought with a price:
> therefore glorify God in your **body**
> and in your spirit, which are God's.
> —I. Cor. vi. 19, 20.

In his letter to the Ephesians the same
writer again mentions this "purchased possession," which certainly means the mortal body,
and refers to its having received an earnest of
the inheritance, in view of the full redemption
that was to come. The earnest of the inheritance is undoubtedly the quickening of the
mortal body by the Spirit. We do not mean
by this an impartation of the physical life of
Christ, but a renewing and quickening of the
body by the Spirit. Scripture bears witness
with the experience of vast multitudes of saints
who have laid hold of this promise of God.
Here again the lower critic is making desperate
attempts to deprive the children of God of the
blessing, by relegating this quickening of the
body to the second coming of Christ. Not
believing in the supernatural for the present,
he is compelled as a consequence to try and
explain it away. Having entrenched himself
in the realm of theory, he cannot humble himself to investigate the realm of experience.
Why should any Christian question the impartation of life for the body when such is
most necessary in many cases to carry on the
work of the Lord? Many saintly servants of
Christ have sought bodily strength through
prayer, and have given astounding testimonies
to their deliverances.

The Marvellous Mortal Body

JOHN WESLEY

must have experienced this quickening of the Spirit in his body, to be able to carry on his strenuous labours. We are definitely told that he was a believer in Divine healing. At one time he was seized with a pain when in the midst of preaching, so that he could no longer speak ; then, uttering the words, " I know my remedy," he immediately kneeled down and was healed. At another time he was taken with pain, cough, and fever so that he became very weak in body. To use his own words, " I called on Jesus aloud to increase my faith, and to confirm the word of His grace. While I was speaking my pain vanished away, my fever left me, and *my bodily strength returned,* and for many weeks I felt neither weariness nor pain. Unto Thee, O Lord, do I give thanks."

In his journals

GEORGE FOX,

the saintly Quaker and founder of the Friends' Society, eloquently testifies to the Spirit of God coming upon him when almost dead. He was at the time preaching at Ulverstone, and as a result of his powerful denunciation of sin the enemy raged, and roused the people to bodily persecution. " Then on a sudden the people were in a rage, and fell upon me in the steeple-house ; they knocked me down, kicked me, and trampled upon me ; and so great was the uproar, that some people tumbled over their seats for fear. They led me about a quarter of

a mile, some taking hold by my collar, and
some by my arms and shoulders, and shook
and dragged me along. Now when they had
haled me to the common-moss side, a multitude of people following, the constables and
other officers gave me some blows over my back
with their willow rods, and so thrust me among
the rude multitude, who, having furnished
themselves, some with staves, some with hedge-
stakes, and others with holm or holly bushes,
fell upon me, and beat me on my head, arms,
and shoulders, till they deprived me of sense,
so that I fell down upon the wet common.
When I recovered again, and saw myself lying
in a watery common, and the people standing
about me, I lay still a little while ; and the
power of the Lord sprang through me, and
the *Eternal Refreshings refreshed me,* so that
I stood up again in the strengthening power
of the Eternal God ; and stretching out my
arms amongst them, I said with a loud voice,
' Strike again ; here are my arms, my head,
and my cheeks.' There was in the company
a mason, a professor, but a rude fellow ; he
with his walking rule-staff gave me a blow with
all his might, just over the back of my hand,
as it was stretched out ; with which blow my
hand was so bruised, and my arm so benumbed,
that I could not draw it unto me again ; so that
some of the people cried out, ' He hath
spoiled his hand for ever having the use of it
any more.' But I looked at it in the love of

God (for I was in the love of God to them all, that had persecuted me) and after a while the Lord's power sprang through me again, and through my hand and arm, so that in a moment I recovered strength in my hand and arm, in the sight of them all."

The testimony of

EVAN ROBERTS,

the Welsh Revivalist, whose memory will ever be enshrined in the heart of the Principality, lost the physical weakness from which he suffered when the Holy Spirit clothed him for his great work.

Describing his experience in the prayer meeting when the power of God came upon him he said, " After many had prayed, *I felt some living energy or force entering my bosom,* restraining my breath, my legs trembling terribly ; this living energy increased and increased as one after the other prayed. Feeling strangely and deeply moved and warmed, I burst forth in prayer." One writing of him said, " He used to get very tired after walking a few miles, but on the above night he walked eight miles from Blaenanerch to Newcastle Emlyn, and felt nothing after it, though he had been ill for four days previously. The day after, he walked five miles without getting at all tired. This is remarkable when we remember that he was almost too weak to walk from the house of the Rev. M. P. Morgan to the chapel, a distance of a few dozen yards, the morning that he was filled with the Spirit. He felt some physical freedom penetrating through his whole body, and the physical impediment to which he was subject previously to this disappeared entirely. He felt a certain difficulty when singing, speaking, or doing other things ; but from the moment he received the Spirit, that was not experienced by him any more.''

PERSONAL TESTIMONY.

Upon entering one of the classrooms when studying for the ministry, I found the following sentence written on the blackboard, '' *He that hath an experience is not at the mercy of him that hath an argument.*'' When I read these words I could not help but say aloud, '' Yes, and especially if the experience carries with it the authority of Scripture.'' I was first convinced of the Spirit's quickening power when, as a frail youth, I received the experience in my own body. My weak state began to manifest itself in facial paralysis, and I was heavily burdened, for I felt the creepiness of paralysis down one whole side. Being somewhat reticent I suffered in silence beyond measure, for I knew that unless a miracle was wrought in me, life was to be very short. When my mouth began to be affected, the one thing that distressed me greatly was the possibility of my not realising the one call and ambition of life, the Christian ministry. From the earliest days of childhood there was that consciousness borne with me that I was called to preach the Gospel. When this affliction came it seemed as if the end of all that was worth living had come, there was no other purpose for me in life if I could not preach. We were kneeling in prayer one Sunday morning and were interceding on the subject of the services of that day. It was exactly nine o'clock when the power of God came upon me, and I received such an inflow of Divine life that I can only liken the experience to being charged with electricity. It seemed as if my head were connected to a *most powerful electric battery.* My whole body from head to foot was quickened by the Spirit of God, and I was healed. From that day I have never had the least symptoms of the old trouble. Many times since then I have relied upon the Spirit's quickening power for my body. All who conduct prolonged evangelistic campaigns will admit that a great deal of physical strength is necessary. This in many cases could never be found if it were not for Divine strength that is given. The body, tired and weakened by constant labour, needs a special inflow of Divine life. Sometimes towards the end of a campaign I have been confronted by monster congregations, and if it were not for the frequent quickening of the body I would have been helpless. Even the voice is charged and changed as the result of the body being quickened by the Spirit. *The difficulty with opposers to this truth generally is that they consult people about these experiences who have never known them.* They make the same kind of mistake that Pilate made, when he asked the frenzied mob who were strangers to Christ, '' What shall I do then with Jesus which is called the Christ? '' If he were to consider for one moment he would have anticipated the answer that was given. Had he turned to Bartimæus who knew Christ, Pilate would have received a different answer, for Jesus had opened his eyes. Had he taken the trouble to consult Mary Magdalene, she would have said, '' Accept Him, Pilate ; He cast seven demons out of me.'' Near by he might have seen the upright woman who was once held in chains of bondage for eighteen years. She would have given him the right answer, for Christ had brought her liberty. Pilate in his day asked advice of the wrong people, just as opposers to this glorious truth in the present day consult the wrong people.

Throughout our land to-day there are multitudes who testify before wondering congregations of their deliverances from all kinds of physical ailments. Cripples who have stepped out of wheeled chairs and carriages are now walking as other people. The paralysed and lame have discarded their crutches, and are confirming their testimonies by walking unaided. Eyes once wrapped in the blackness and darkness of midnight now see the light of glorious day. Deaf ears, shut in with a strange and unnatural silence, now respond to sweet music and the singing of the birds. Bodies weary and worn by various diseases have been quickened, relieved, and delivered. The oppressed, crushed by ever-increasing burdens, have been uplifted and raised. Thus the testimonies go forth while the manifested healings and miracles confirm.

The happenings of to-day are akin to those we read of in the Bible. The healings of to-day are exactly like those of the days of the apostles. Neither should God's people be surprised, for the Divine Healer of this the twentieth century is the One who healed in the first. Just as in the Acts of the Apostles, the effect upon the mortal bodies of those touched by the Healer Divine is the same. The lame man of chapter iii. received such a manifestation in his body when healed that he was found walking, leaping, and praising God. Æneas of chapter ix., who was bedridden for eight years with palsy, was raised and made whole, and all that dwelt at Lydda and Saron saw him and turned to the Lord. The cripple of chapter xiv. who was impotent in his feet and had never walked, must have received a quickening of his mortal body, when he was seen standing, walking, and leaping. Paul the apostle in the same chapter must have received a wonderful quickening, when raised after being apparently stoned to death. Again, in chapter xxviii. it must have been the quickening of the mortal body that saved him from the deadly poison of the viper.

THE MORTAL BODY A TEMPLE OF THE HOLY SPIRIT.

> But ye shall receive power after that the Holy Ghost is come upon you : and ye shall be witnesses unto Me both in Jerusalem, and in all Judæa, and in Samaria, and unto the uttermost part of the earth.—Acts i. 8.
>
> He that believeth on Me, as the Scripture hath said, out of his belly shall flow rivers of living water.
>
> But this spake He of the Spirit, which they that believe on Him should receive. . , .—John vii. 38, 39.

The presentation of this truth by teachers of different schools has caused much confusion of thought among the Lord's people, one declaring that the Baptism of the Holy Spirit is received at conversion, another that it is the birthright of the believer and can only be received by those already converted. Teachers also differ as to what is experienced by the recipients of the Baptism of the Holy Spirit. One claims that it is received by faith without any manifestation whatever. Another maintains that the Baptism of the Holy Spirit results in physical manifestations. The purpose for which the Baptism is given is also differently explained. Some teach that it means a full consecration on the part of the believer, when sin within is absolutely destroyed. Others that the Baptism of the Spirit can only be received by those who are already delivered from all sin, and that it is given to empower witnesses for service. My purpose here is not to discuss these different views, but to consider the one great truth that all are agreed upon, namely, that the body is the temple of the Holy Ghost.

Let us look at a few instances in the New Testament where the Holy Spirit was received. The first great outpouring took place on the Day of Pentecost when one hundred and twenty individuals received. These disciples were empowered, and the power manifested itself through their mortal bodies. They were all filled with the Holy Ghost, and began to speak with other tongues, as the Spirit gave them utterance. Their mortal bodies were filled and visibly affected by the incoming Spirit. The next great outpouring occurred at Samaria where Philip the evangelist laboured. The baptised and joyous converts in this revival had hands laid upon them for the reception of the Holy Spirit. They too were visibly affected as the incoming Spirit took control of their mortal bodies. Simon must have witnessed this manifestation, for he offered to purchase the power. Another outpouring of the Spirit took place at the specially convened meeting at the house of Cornelius. Here again manifestations were given which revealed the effect of the Spirit upon those who received as they listened to Peter. Undoubtedly when the Holy Spirit comes in He manifests Himself in the mortal bodies of all who receive. There is no reason for supposing that He has changed in His manner of working, even in our day. Out of the innermost being rivers of living water will flow.

THE MORTAL BODY BECOMES IMMORTAL.

> For our conversation is in heaven; from whence also we look for the Saviour, the Lord Jesus Christ,
> Who shall change this body of our humiliation that it may be fashioned like unto the body of His glory.—Phil. iii. 20, 21.

We have already seen that the mortal body becomes a servant of righteousness at salvation, is quickened when healed, and is empowered for service at the Baptism of the Holy Spirit. We shall now consider how it will be affected at the coming of our Lord. Paul in his letter to the Corinthians graphically describes what will happen to the body at the second advent of Christ. "We shall all be changed, in a moment, in the twinkling of an eye"; and "this mortal shall put on immortality." The term *mortal* as we have seen means "subject to death," and it can only refer to those who are alive. Believers who are alive when Christ comes shall put on immortality. The dead in Christ will, of course, be raised at the same time, but they put on incorruption. The mortal body of the believer will be absorbed by the life of the Lord, and he shall not taste of death. What a glorious event to look forward to ! What a glorious thought to ponder over ! What a manifestation of power to witness !

The glory of the King's advent shall be seen by the once blind eye, and the sound of the trumpet shall break in upon the ear that used to be deaf. The weak shall be made strong, and every sick one healed. Like the hosts who were delivered miraculously from the land of Egypt, there shall not be a single feeble person among the raptured saints at the second advent of Christ. Until He comes we shall continue to praise Him for the earnest of that glorious inheritance, and wait patiently and prayerfully for the full redemption of the purchased possession, which includes the mortal body. During the waiting time we are citizens of heaven and must live as such before our fellow men. We are ambassadors representing the court of heaven down here, and we must never lower the dignity of that calling. We are here carrying on the work He has graciously allotted to us, and we must occupy till He comes. It has pleased God to bestow abundant honour upon our mortal bodies by making them His dwelling place, filling and quickening them in the present age.

CHAPTER VI

Bodily Healing in the Dispensation of the Father

Bless the Lord, O my soul, and forget not all His benefits: who forgiveth all thine iniquities; who healeth all thy diseases.—Psalm ciii. 2, 3.

BODILY healing in answer to prayer abounds in the dispensation of type and shadow. Old Testament saints experienced the deliverance from bodily ailments as well as the deliverance from sin, as we shall see in this chapter. To them both deliverances were the immediate benefits of the atoning and redeeming work of Christ on the cross which they saw mirrored in their sacrifices.

A PATRIARCH'S PRAYER ANSWERED.

> So Abraham prayed unto God: and God healed Abimelech, and his wife, and his maidservants.—Genesis xx. 17.

The first case of miraculous healing in the Patriarchal dispensation mentioned in the Bible was wrought in answer to the prayer of father Abraham.

ONE HUNDRED AND TWENTY YEARS OLD.

> And Moses was an hundred and twenty years old when he died : his eye was not dim, nor his natural force abated.
>
> And the children of Israel wept for Moses in the plains of Moab thirty days : so the days of weeping and mourning for Moses were ended.
>
> And there arose not a prophet since in Israel like unto Moses, whom the Lord knew face to face.
>
> In all the signs and the wonders, which the Lord sent him to do in the land of Egypt to Pharaoh, and to all his servants, and to all his land.—Deut. xxxiv. 7, 8, 10, 11.

Moses, who recorded this early testimony to Divine healing had a most remarkable experience of the working of the supernatural in his own body.

ISRAEL AN A1 GRADE NATION,

> He brought them forth also with silver and gold : and there was not one feeble person among their tribes.
> —Psalm cv. 37.

Apart from the supernatural it would be impossible to account for the splendid state of bodily preservation in which the whole nation of Israel found themselves when they were delivered from Egypt. Their long-drawn-out agony through previous years of suffering, the affliction of cruel taskmasters, and the bondage of the tyrant must have made inroads in the health and the constitution of the strongest amongst them. Their backs must have been lacerated by the cruel and frequent whippings, their bodies weakened as a result of the forced and rigorous labour, and the bitterness of life must have been almost unbearable, for their groans entered into the ears of the Lord of sabaoth. No more graphic description of a subdued and suffering people could be given than that found in the record of Exodus : " I have surely seen the affliction of My people which are in Egypt, and have heard their cry by reason of their taskmasters ; for I know their sorrows." The conditions under which they lived must have reduced their mortal frames to a state much below normal, and it is easy to conclude that there were some amongst that great company, estimated at two million folk, who were feeble and diseased, yet the inspired Psalmist declares Israel as a whole to be an A1 grade nation.

THE GREAT HEALING COVENANT.

And when they came to Marah, they could not drink of the waters of Marah, for they were bitter : therefore the name of it was called Marah.

And the people murmured against Moses, saying, What shall we drink?

And he cried unto the Lord ; and the Lord shewed him a tree, which when he had cast into the waters, the waters were made sweet : there

> He made for them a statute and an
> ordinance, and there He proved them.
> And said, , . . I will put none of
> these diseases upon thee, which I
> have brought upon the Egyptians :
> for I am the Lord that healeth thee.
> —Exodus xv. 23-26.

The children of Israel, having been delivered
from Egypt, had just crossed the Red Sea
when this striking healing covenant was made.
To us who live in the twentieth century the
events that preceded its announcement are full
of typical import. Egypt is seen as the world
of sin in which we were held captive, the blood
of a lamb upon the lintel and sideposts of each
house typifies the blood of the Lamb on the
Cross by which we have been delivered. The
journeyings of the Israelites which immediately
followed their deliverance from Egypt is typical
of our earthly pilgrimage towards the better
land. The Israelites were given to understand,
almost at the commencement of their wilderness
journeyings, that bodily healing was a benefit
they could claim from Jehovah, provided they
would comply with the conditions that were attached to the glorious promise. We who have
been " born again," and are on our way to
our heavenly Father's home, are also given to
understand that bodily healing is a present-day
benefit of the last Adam's obedience.   Three
days' journeyings through a tropical country
bring the murmuring Israelites to Marah, and
instead of being able to quench a burning thirst,

it is accentuated by the bitterness of its waters.
Moses their leader, loses no time in seeking
Divine intervention and prays unto the Lord.
In answer to his prayer guidance is given, and
a tree is cast into the waters which changed
the nature of the water, and made it refreshing
and invigorating to drink. Whether this is
healing in the supernatural or natural realm is
a burning question which is much discussed by
those who are, respectively, for and against the
truth of Divine healing. On the one hand it
is maintained that the tree in this instance was
akin to a tree with remedial properties that has
been discovered, which counteracts the deadly
effects of malaria in tropical countries. On the
other hand there are some who rule out the
idea of the tree which healed the waters of
Marah having natural remedial properties.
They maintain that the last words of the pas-
sage, namely, '' I am the Lord that healeth
thee,'' reveal the striking parable that under-
lies the incident—the waters represent the
people, the bitterness speaks of sickness which
embitters life, the tree foreshadowed Calvary,
with the Saviour bearing the curse on the tree
of the Cross. We do not see that it serves any
useful purpose to enter into a controversy of
this kind, for we have already shewn that
there is nothing incompatible between healing
in the realm of the supernatural and healing in
the realm of the natural. The one thing we
can be definite about is that healing came to

the waters of Marah after Moses had cried unto
the Lord. We shall now consider the conditions that are attached to Old Testament promises of bodily healing.

REQUISITE CONDITIONS.

> If thou wilt diligently hearken to
> the voice of the Lord thy God, and
> wilt do that which is right in His
> sight, and wilt give ear to His com-
> mandments, and keep all His
> statutes, I will put none of these
> diseases upon thee, which I have
> brought upon the Egyptians : for I
> am the Lord that healeth thee.—
> Exodus xv. 26.

The conditions under which the saints of the
Old Testament could claim bodily healing included the keeping of the moral law, the ceremonial laws, and the laws which governed the
physical condition of the people. All of which
are applicable to the saints of the twentieth
century, except those that have served their
day and are definitely ruled out in the New
Testament. Saints of the Old Testament had
to observe the conditions under which the great
healing covenant operated. They were granted
a law of immunity from the prevalent diseases
that surrounded them, and the little word " if, "
though only of two letters, was the key that
unlocked the sluices and allowed the free flow
of Divine healing and health in their day.

OBEDIENCE TO THE MORAL LAW.

> . . . . If thou wilt diligently hearken to the voice of the Lord thy God, and wilt do that which is right in His sight, and wilt give ear to His commandments, and keep all His statutes, I will put none of these diseases upon thee . . .—Exodus xv. 26.

Obedience to God's moral law was the ground on which the children of Israel could claim bodily healing. The breaking of the moral law has, throughout the history of the human race, been visited with all kinds of bodily afflictions that are both fearful and loathsome. Sin, which is defined in the New Testament as " the transgression of the law," is the cause of all evil from which mortals have suffered. The great healing covenant meant to the Israelites relief from its awful consequences and immunity from sickness and disease, provided they complied with the conditions that were attached to it. There is something significant about the circumstances under which this great healing covenant was made. Based upon obedience, it was given just at the commencement of a new life into which the children of Israel had entered. They had just crossed over from a land that was noted for its knowledge of medical science. It was in that land, so famous for this particular branch of science, that Moses, the divinely chosen leader of the people, was trained. In it he was thoroughly educated, for the New Testament declares that " Moses was learned in all the wisdom of the Egyptians." Having been trained in its wisdom it is not beyond the bounds of possibility that he was a fully quali-fied physician. A person with the educational accomplishments such as he possessed must have acquired the highest possible information along these lines. It is only reasonable to presume that Moses was skilled to a very high degree in the science for which the land had become famous. Yet the source of healing was not declared to be in Moses but in God. " I am the Lord that healeth thee," was the Divine declaration in the palmy plains of Elim. God there pledged Himself to be the Healer of His people, and that pledge was confirmed by the revelation of His Name. It was the guarantee that accompanied the promise of healing. We often find that when God wanted to reveal Himself as being able to meet a particular need, He did so by clothing Himself with a title that expressed His ability to do so. Hence we have the various titles of Jehovah through-out the whole of Scripture. For instance :

JEHOVAH-JIREH : THE LORD WILL PROVIDE.

And Abraham lifted up his eyes, and looked, and behold behind him a ram caught in a thicket by his horns : and Abraham went and took the ram, and offered him up for a burnt offering in the stead of his son.

71

> And Abraham called the name of
> that place Jehovah-Jireh : as it is said
> to this day, In the mount of the Lord
> it shall be seen.—Genesis xxii. 13, 14.

Father Abraham well understood the meaning of this title when he ascended Mount Moriah for the purpose of sacrificing his only son. He also knew that Isaac dead would mean the end of all the promises, whereas Isaac alive meant the fulfilment of all. Yet he went forth in faith, believing that God would keep His word, even to the extent of raising Isaac from the dead. Acquaintance with God, whose Name revealed His power and willingness to provide, encouraged him in the pathway of obedience. Faith in Jehovah-Jireh furnished the answer to Isaac's question as they walked towards the place of sacrifice—" My son, God will provide Himself a lamb for a burnt-offering."

JEHOVAH-TSIDKENU : THE LORD OUR RIGHTEOUSNESS.

> Behold, the days come, saith the
> Lord, that I will raise unto David a
> righteous Branch, and a King shall
> reign and prosper, and shall execute
> judgment and justice in the earth.
> In His days Judah shall be saved,
> and Israel shall dwell safely : and
> this is His name whereby He shall
> be called, The Lord our righteous-
> ness.—Jer. xxiii. 5, 6.

This is the name of the King who shall reign over the whole earth in days that are soon to come. Every believer in Christ should greatly value this name, because it ensures a future Millennium. We in the British Empire certainly value our citizenship, for we have been privileged to come under the reigns of noble potentates. We have enjoyed blessings that seem to have been denied our less fortunate brethren who are citizens of other lands. The name British, which means " covenant man," appears to be the guarantee of goodwill, and the Union Jack a symbol of good government. But at present the whole world lieth in the lap of the Evil One ; sin is rampant, disease and death are stalking throughout the earth, plagues are preying upon humanity, there are wars and rumours of wars, and the shadows of the great tribulation are hovering over the whole world. It would indeed be a sad outlook if it were not for the great change that is soon to take place. Jesus the Saviour is to become Christ the King. He is to reign on a literal throne on this literal earth, when evil will be superseded by goodness, unrest by tranquillity, and unrighteousness by righteousness. Our precious Lord, who bears the glorious title, Jehovah-Tsidkenu, is to reign supreme.

JEHOVAH-ROPHI : THE LORD THAT HEALETH.

. . . For I am the Lord that healeth thee.—Exodus xv, 26.

73

That this refers to bodily healing the context clearly shews, and the Israelites could not possibly understand it to mean anything else. It pleased God at this time to clothe Himself with a name that revealed the power and will to heal them of their bodily diseases. They were not to depend upon the medical knowledge which their leader Moses must have possessed, for medical science at its best is imperfect. It has made serious blunders and stupendous mistakes. In this as in all other realms of science, opinions continually change and the supposed certainties of yesterday are the certain inaccuracies of to-day. In so far as it harmonises with the natural law which God has graciously bestowed upon the whole of mankind, it is to be appreciated. The Israelites understood that deliverance from all bodily ailments was by the power of God, that immunity from disease was a privilege they could enjoy provided they rendered perfect obedience to His will.

OBEDIENCE TO THE CEREMONIAL LAW.

And the Lord spake unto Moses, saying,

This shall be the law of the leper in the day of his cleansing: he shall be brought unto the priest:

And the priest shall go forth out of the camp; and the priest shall look, and, behold, if the plague of leprosy be healed in the leper;

> Then shall the priest command to take for him that is to be cleansed two birds alive and clean, and cedar wood, and scarlet, and hyssop :
>
> And the priest shall command that one of the birds be killed in an earthen vessel over running water.
>
> As for the living bird, he shall take it, and the cedar wood, and the scarlet, and the hyssop, and shall dip them and the living bird in the blood of the bird that was killed over the running water :
>
> And he shall sprinkle upon him that is to be cleansed from the leprosy seven times, and shall pronounce him clean, and shall let the living bird loose into the open field.
>
> —Lev. xiv. 1-7.

This cleansing of the leper was closely associated with a law of ceremonies that foreshadowed the blessings that came through redemption. The leper, a type of the sinner, wends his way to the priest, and, after humbly confessing his uncleanness, participates in a ceremony that vividly typifies the death and resurrection of Christ. The ceremonial passed away when Christ came, for He was the end of every whit of that law. The type passed away when the antitype came, the shadow disappeared in the substance, and the picture was obliterated by the appearance of the real. The writer of the Epistle to the Hebrews fully realised this when he declared :

> For the law having a shadow of good things to come, and not the very image of the things, can never with those sacrifices which they offered year by year continually make the comers thereunto perfect.—Heb. x. 1.

OBEDIENCE TO NATURAL LAWS OF HEALTH.

> Command the children of Israel, that they put out of the camp every leper, and every one that hath an issue, and whosoever is defiled by the dead :
>
> Both male and female shall ye put out, without the camp shall ye put them ; that they defile not their camps, in the midst whereof I dwell.
>
> And the children of Israel did so, and put them without the camp : as the Lord spake unto Moses, so did the children of Israel.—Num. v. 2-4.

The above scripture is but one instance of the way in which the children of Israel obeyed laws governing their physical condition. The rules of hygiene and sanitary science which God gave to Israel in her wilderness journeyings are as stringent as those which operate in any military camp. In fact, many of the methods for preservation of health and the prevention of disease are very similar. Almost four thousand years of civilisation have not improved upon those God-given methods, and much more can still be learned from them to-day. One may see similar schemes at work in any Territorial camp. There are solitary huts or tents at a conspicuous distance from the camp, where those who have, or are suspected of having, infectious diseases are isolated. The high standard of cleanliness of person, clothes, dwelling places, and all equipment of a military camp is a replica of the healthful manner of living imposed upon the Israelites. These age-long rules, if obeyed by the spiritual Israel of the twentieth century, would ensure the highest possible standard of health. They are old but ever new.

We shall now consider some definite cases of healing in the dispensation of the Father.

A PLAGUE WAS STAYED.

And Moses said unto Aaron, Take a censer, and put fire therein from off the altar, and put on incense, and go quickly unto the congregation, and make an atonement for them : for there is wrath gone out from the Lord; the plague is begun.

And Aaron took as Moses commanded, and ran into the midst of the congregation; and, behold, the plague was begun among the people : and he put on incense, and made an atonement for the people.

And he stood between the dead and the living; and the plague was stayed.—Num. xvi. 46-48.

77

On this occasion the children of Israel murmured against the divinely appointed leaders of the people, and there was much dissatisfaction throughout the camp. Open rebellion had broken out, which called for extraordinary and immediate discipline, for the whole future of their civilisation was in danger of being torn to shreds. Their sin caused the great plague, which overtook them in an alarming manner, until they were horror-stricken. With his usual foresight and faith Moses commands Aaron to make an atonement for them, and the high priest, making atonement, stands between the living and the dead. God miraculously intervened and the plague was stayed.

LEPROSY HEALED.

And the cloud departed from off the tabernacle; and, behold, Miriam became leprous, white as snow: and Aaron looked upon Miriam, and, behold, she was leprous,

And Aaron said unto Moses, Alas, my lord, I beseech thee, lay not the sin upon us, wherein we have done foolishly, and wherein we have sinned . . .

And Moses cried unto the Lord, saying, Heal her now, O God, I beseech Thee . . .

And Miriam was shut out from the camp seven days: and the people journeyed not till Miriam was brought in again.—Num. xii. 10, 11, 13, 15.

" Jealousy is cruel as the grave : the coals thereof are coals of fire, which hath a most vehement flame.'' Such is the description of this terrible sin given by the inspired writer. Miriam, in conjunction with Aaron her brother, had nursed jealousy in her heart, and had spoken unwisely against Moses. Such indiscretion brought about the loathsome disease that has always been used as a type of sin. She was brought to judgment, and condemned right in the presence of Moses, against whom she had transgressed. In response to Aaron's request Moses immediately sought the Lord for his sister's forgiveness and healing. The Word does not say that she was healed instantaneously, but it does say she was restored to the camp at the end of one week. Her marvellous healing came in direct answer to prayer.

BLOOD-POISONING HEALED.

Therefore the people came to Moses, and said, We have sinned, for we have spoken against the Lord, and against thee; pray unto the Lord, that He take away the serpents from us. And Moses prayed for the people.

And the Lord said unto Moses, Make thee a fiery serpent, and set it upon a pole : and it shall come to pass, that everyone that is bitten, when he looketh upon it, shall live.

And Moses made a serpent of

brass, and put it upon a pole, and it
came to pass, that if a serpent had
bitten any man, when he beheld the
serpent of brass, he lived.—Num.
xxi. 7-9.

Here again we find murmuring in the camp
of Israel. They had become dissatisfied, and
were openly speaking against Moses and
Aaron. It was this sin that brought the fiery
serpents with poisonous bite into their midst.
They were bitten by these fiery serpents as
a distinct judgment because of their sin, and
were dying of blood-poisoning. After confessing their sin Moses held aloft the pole
with the brazen serpent, and encouraged the
Israelites to look thereon and be healed. Deliverance came in answer to the prayer of
Moses, and they were miraculously healed.
The Lord Jesus Christ, about fifteen hundred
years after this event, had occasion to preach
salvation to one called Nicodemus from this
uplifted brazen serpent. Thus it foreshadowed
the atoning and redeeming work of the uplifted
Christ as the sovereign remedy for all the evil
effects of sin. In all the three cases of healing
to which we have referred, deliverances were
given as a result of true heart repentance.

JEROBOAM'S WITHERED HAND WAS HEALED.

And it came to pass, when King
Jeroboam heard the saying of the
man of God, which had cried against

the altar in Bethel, that he put forth
his hand from the altar, saying, Lay
hold on him. And his hand, which
he put forth against him, dried up,
so that he could not pull it in again
to him . . .

And the king answered and said
unto the man of God, Intreat now
the face of the Lord thy God, and
pray for me, that my hand may be
restored me again. And the man of
God besought the Lord, and the
king's hand was restored him again,
and became as it was before.—I.
Kings xiii. 4, 6.

FIFTEEN YEARS ADDED TO HEZEKIAH'S LIFE.

And it came to pass, afore Isaiah
was gone out into the middle court,
that the word of the Lord came to
him, saying,

Turn again, and tell Hezekiah the
captain of My people, Thus saith the
Lord, the God of David thy father,
I have heard thy prayer, I have seen
thy tears: behold, I will heal thee:
on the third day thou shalt go up unto
the house of the Lord.

And I will add unto thy days fifteen years . . .

And Isaiah said, Take a lump of
figs. And they took and laid it on
the boil, and he recovered.—II. Kings
xx. 4-7.

CHILD WHO DIED OF SUNSTROKE RAISED.

And when the child was grown, it fell on a day, that he went out to his father to the reapers.

And he said unto his father, My head, my head. And he said to a lad, Carry him to his mother.

And when he had taken him, and brought him to his mother, he sat on her knees till noon, and then died.

And when Elisha was come into the house, behold, the child was dead, and laid upon his bed.

Then he returned, and walked in the house to and fro; and went up, and stretched himself upon him: and the child sneezed seven times, and the child opened his eyes.—II. Kings iv. 18-20, 32, 35.

NAAMAN WAS HEALED OF LEPROSY.

Now Naaman, captain of the host of the King of Syria, was a great man with his master, and honourable, because by him the Lord had given deliverance unto Syria: he was also a mighty man in valour, but he was a leper.

Then went he down, and dipped himself seven times in Jordan, according to the saying of the man of God: and his flesh came again like unto the flesh of a little child, and he was clean.

And he returned to the man of God, he and all his company, and came, and stood before him: and he said,

Behold, now I know that there is
no God in all the earth, but in Israel.
—II. Kings v. 1, 14, 15.

JOB WAS HEALED OF BOILS.

So went Satan forth from the presence of the Lord, and smote Job
with sore boils from the sole of his
foot unto his crown.—Job ii. 7.

And the Lord turned the captivity
of Job, when he prayed for his
friends : also the Lord gave Job
twice as much as he had before.—
Job xlii. 10.

NEBUCHADNEZZAR WAS HEALED OF INSANITY.

The same hour was the thing fulfilled upon Nebuchadnezzar : and he
was driven from men, and did eat
grass as oxen, and his body was wet
with the dew of heaven, till his hairs
were grown like eagles' feathers,
and his nails like birds' claws.

And at the end of the days I
Nebuchadnezzar lifted up mine eyes
unto heaven, and mine understanding returned unto me, and I blessed
the most High, and I praised and
honoured Him that liveth for ever,
whose dominion is an everlasting
dominion, and His kingdom is from
generation to generation.—Daniel
iv. 33, 34.

In face of all the testimonies of healing that
are given in the Old Testament it would be
more than futile to try and deny that those who

lived in the dispensation of the Father, and who obeyed His Word, enjoyed complete immunity from diseases and sickness of all kinds. As long as they obeyed, they had a right to claim bodily healing and bodily health. When they disobeyed, they were afflicted and suffered in body. In their bodily afflictions they were commanded to turn to the Lord, from whom they could claim bodily healing, provided they complied with the conditions that were attached to God's promises of healing.

Solomon testifies to the fulfilment of God's promises :

> Blessed be the Lord, that hath given rest unto His people Israel, according to all that He promised : there hath not failed one word of all His good promise, which He promised by the hand of Moses His servant. —I. Kings viii. 56.

The testimony of Joshua also appears thus :

> And, behold, this day I am going the way of all the earth: and ye know in all your hearts and in all your souls, that not one thing hath failed of all the good things which the Lord your God spake concerning you; all are come to pass unto you, and not one thing hath failed thereof.—Joshua xxiii. 14.

CHAPTER VII

Bodily Healing in the Dispensation of the Son

And Jesus went about all Galilee, teaching in their synagogues, and preaching the Gospel of the kingdom, and healing all manner of sickness and all manner of disease among the people.—Matt. iv. 23.

How God anointed Jesus of Nazareth with the Holy Ghost and with power: who went about doing good, and healing all that were oppressed of the devil; for God was with Him.—Acts x. 38.

INSPIRED history has faithfully recorded the many and great miracles that accompanied the ministry of Jesus of Nazareth. Yet, in spite of conclusive proof produced, there are those in our day who try to explain these miracles away. They are the enemies of the true Christian religion, and they know that if they can succeed in divesting Christianity of that which is essential to establish its claims, they will have destroyed the whole. Christianity stripped of the miraculous means that there was no Virgin birth, and thus its foundation has gone; that Jesus of Nazareth was only a man, hence His Deity is taken away; that He died on the cross of Calvary as a martyr, consequently there was no atonement made; that

85

He was not raised from the dead, hence all faith in Christianity is in vain. Those who try to explain away the miracles in the life of Christ are undermining the New Testament. It is consoling to know that it would be far easier to drain the ocean dry with a teaspoon than to destroy the least part of the inspired Word. It would be much easier to bring the East and the West together than to take away one single jot or tittle. The immediate interposition of God in laws that were contrary to and above nature more than confirmed the Divine mission of Christ before all the people. This is exemplified by the statement that our Lord made to those whom John the Baptist had deputed to wait upon Him. The work of the forerunner had been accomplished; the tongue that had heralded forth the message of preparation was about to be silenced; the light that had flickered in the desert had served its purpose,— for the Source of all light had come, and he who was destined to decrease at the appearance of Christ was within prison walls. One can easily imagine what thoughts were passing through his mind—"What meaneth this? Was I not divinely called to prepare the way of the Lord? Why am I in prison, and yet there is no sign of His appearance? Surely there must be a mistake somewhere; my mission cannot be over, for the One who was to increase has not appeared?" These were the questions that must have been crowding in upon the Baptist, the prisoner of Herod. Then news began to be circulated concerning one called Jesus who had appeared upon the scene, and there were further questionings. " Is it possible that this Jesus is the One I have been looking for? If so, why does He allow me to be in prison ?" The light of hope shines in his eyes, and he is determined to find the answer to all his questionings. Two of his faithful followers are deputed to visit the scene of this Nazarene's labours, and to put the all-important question to Him.

THE DIVINE CREDENTIALS.

Now when John had heard in the prison the works of Christ, he sent two of his disciples,

And said unto Him, Art Thou He that should come, or do we look for another?

Jesus answered and said unto them, Go and shew John again those things which ye do hear and see :

The blind receive their sight, and the lame walk, the lepers are cleansed, and the deaf hear, the dead are raised up, and the poor have the Gospel preached to them.

And blessed is he, whosoever shall not be offended in Me.—Matt. xi. 2-6.

Our blessed Lord healed people of all kinds of diseases, and also in some cases raised the dead. Sufferers of all kinds drew freely from

the deep well of His compassionate heart. By
His word lepers were cleansed, blind eyes made
to see, deaf ears were unstopped, the tongue
of the dumb was loosed, cripples began to walk,
and paralysed limbs were made perfectly whole.
He was indeed touched with the feelings and
infirmities of suffering humanity at every turn.

The following tabulated cases will demon-
strate remarkable healings of various diseases
in the ministry of our Lord.

ONE HEALED OF LEPROSY.

And, behold, there came a leper
and worshipped Him, saying, Lord,
if Thou wilt, Thou canst make me
clean.
And Jesus put forth His hand, and
touched him, saying, I will; be thou
clean. And immediately his leprosy
was cleansed.—Matt. viii. 2, 3.

PETER'S MOTHER-IN-LAW HEALED OF FEVER.

And when Jesus was come into
Peter's house, He saw his wife's
mother laid, and sick of a fever.
And He touched her hand, and
the fever left her: and she arose, and
ministered unto them.—Matt. viii.
14, 15.

REMARKABLE HEALINGS IN ONE EVENING.

When the even was come, they
brought unto Him many that were
possessed with devils: and He cast

out the spirits with His word, and healed all that were sick :

That it might be fulfilled which was spoken by Esaias the prophet, saying, Himself took our infirmities, and bare our sicknesses.—Matt. viii. 16, 17.

CENTURION'S SERVANT HEALED OF PALSY.

Lord, my servant lieth at home sick of the palsy, grievously tormented.

And Jesus saith unto him, I will come and heal him.

The centurion answered and said, Lord, I am not worthy that Thou shouldest come under my roof : but speak the word only, and my servant shall be healed.

And Jesus said unto the centurion, Go thy way; and as thou hast believed, so be it done unto thee. And his servant was healed in the selfsame hour.—Matt. viii. 6-8, 13.

A MAN'S WITHERED HAND HEALED.

And, behold, there was a man which had his hand withered.

Then saith He to the man, Stretch forth thine hand. And he stretched it forth : and it was restored whole, like as the other.—Matt. xii. 10, 13.

A LUNATIC HEALED.

And when they were come to the multitude, there came to Him a certain man, kneeling down to Him, and saying,

Lord, have mercy on my son: for he is lunatick, and sore vexed: for ofttimes he falleth into the fire, and oft into the water.

And Jesus rebuked the devil; and he departed out of him: and the child was cured from that very hour. —Matt. xvii. 14, 15, 18.

A DEAF AND DUMB MAN HEALED.

And they bring unto Him one that was deaf, and had an impediment in his speech; and they beseech Him to put His hand upon him.

And He took him aside from the multitude, and put His fingers into his ears, and He spit, and touched his tongue;

And looking up to heaven, he sighed, and saith unto him, Ephphatha, that is, Be opened.

And straightway his ears were opened, and the string of his tongue was loosed, and he spake plain.

And He charged them that they should tell no man: but the more He charged them, so much the more a great deal they published it;

And were beyond measure astonished, saying, He hath done all things well.: He maketh both the deaf to hear, and the dumb to speak. —Mark vii. 32-37.

A BLIND MAN HEALED.

And He cometh to Bethsaida; and they bring a blind man unto Him, and besought Him to touch him.

And He took the blind man by the hand, and led him out of the town; and when He had spit on his eyes, and put His hands upon him, He asked him if he saw ought.

And he looked up, and said, I see men as trees, walking.

After that He put His hands again upon his eyes, and made him look up: and he was restored, and saw every man clearly.—Mark viii. 22-25.

A PARALYSED MAN HEALED.

And, behold, men brought in a bed a man which was taken with a palsy: and they sought means to bring him in, and to lay him before Him.

And when they could not find by what way they might bring him in because of the multitude, they went upon the housetop, and let him down through the tiling with his couch into the midst before Jesus.

But that ye may know that the Son of man hath power upon earth to forgive sins, (He said unto the sick of the palsy,) I say unto thee, Arise, and take up thy couch, and go into thine house.

And immediately he rose up before them, and took up that whereon he lay, and departed to his own house, glorifying God.

And they were all amazed, and they glorified God, and were filled with fear, saying, We have seen strange things to-day.—Luke v. 18, 19, 24-26.

A DEMON-POSSESSED MAN DELIVERED.

And when He went forth to land, there met Him out of the city a certain man, which had devils long time, and ware no clothes, neither abode in any house, but in the tombs.

Then went the devils out of the man, and entered into the swine: and the herd ran violently down a steep place into the lake, and were choked.

Then they went out to see what was done; and came to Jesus, and found the man, out of whom the devils were departed, sitting at the feet of Jesus, clothed, and in his right mind.—Luke viii. 27, 33, 35.

A WOMAN HEALED AFTER TWELVE YEARS' SUFFERING.

And a woman having an issue of blood twelve years, which had spent all her living upon physicians, neither could be healed of any,

And Jesus said, Somebody hath touched Me: for I perceive that virtue is gone out of Me.

And when the woman saw that she was not hid, she came trembling, and falling down before Him, she declared unto Him before all the people for what cause she had touched Him, and how she was healed immediately. Luke viii. 43, 46, 47.

A CROOKED WOMAN MADE STRAIGHT.

And He was teaching in one of the synagogues on the sabbath.

And, behold, there was a woman

which had a spirit of infirmity eighteen years, and was bowed together, and could in no wise lift up herself.

And when Jesus saw her, He called her to Him, and said unto her, Woman, thou art loosed from thine infirmity.

And He laid His hands on her: and immediately she was made straight, and glorified God.—Luke xiii. 10-13.

A MAN HEALED OF DROPSY.

And, behold, there was a certain man before Him which had the dropsy.

And Jesus answering spake unto the lawyers and Pharisees, saying, Is it lawful to heal on the sabbath day?

And they held their peace. And He took him, and healed him, and let him go.—Luke xiv. 2-4.

TEN LEPERS HEALED.

And as He entered into a certain village, there met Him ten men that were lepers, which stood afar off,

And they lifted up their voices, and said, Jesus, Master, have mercy on us.

And when He saw them, He said unto them, Go shew yourselves unto the priests. And it came to pass, that, as they went, they were cleansed.

And one of them, when he saw

that he was healed, turned back, and with a loud voice glorified God. —Luke xvii. 12-15.

EAR RESTORED TO HIGH PRIEST'S SERVANT.

And one of them smote the servant of the high priest, and cut off his right ear.

And Jesus answered and said, Suffer ye thus far. And He touched his ear, and healed him.—Luke xxii. 50, 51.

A NOBLEMAN'S DYING SON HEALED.

So Jesus came again into Cana of Galilee, where He made the water wine. And there was a certain nobleman, whose son was sick at Capernaum.

When He heard that Jesus was come out of Judæa into Galilee, he went unto Him, and besought Him that He would come down, and heal his son: for he was at the point of death.

The nobleman saith unto Him, Sir, come down ere my child die.

Jesus saith unto him, Go thy way; thy son liveth. And the man believed the word that Jesus had spoken unto him, and he went his way.

And as he was now going down, his servants met him, and told him, saying, Thy son liveth.

Then enquired he of them the hour when he began to amend. And they said unto him. Yesterday at the seventh hour the fever left him.— John iv. 46, 47, 49-52.

A CRIPPLE HEALED.

And a certain man was there, which had an infirmity thirty and eight years.

When Jesus saw him lie, and knew that he had been now a long time in that case, He saith unto him, Wilt thou be made whole?

The impotent man answered Him, Sir, I have no man, when the water is troubled, to put me into the pool: but while I am coming, another steppeth down before me.

Jesus saith unto him, Rise, take up thy bed, and walk.

And immediately the man was made whole, and took up his bed, and walked.—John v. 5-9.

LAZARUS RAISED FROM THE DEAD.

Then they took away the stone from the place where the dead was laid. And Jesus lifted up his eyes, and said, Father, I thank Thee that Thou hast heard Me.

And I knew that Thou hearest Me always: but because of the people which stand by I said it, that they may believe that Thou hast sent Me.

And when He thus had spoken, He cried with a loud voice, Lazarus, come forth.

And he that was dead came forth, bound hand and foot with grave-clothes: and his face was bound about with a napkin. Jesus said unto them, Loose him, and let him go.—John xi. 41-44.

GREAT MULTITUDES HEALED.

And great multitudes came unto Him, having with them those that were lame, blind, dumb, maimed, and many others, and cast them down at Jesus' feet; and He healed them :

Insomuch that the multitude wondered, when they saw the dumb to speak, the maimed to be whole, the lame to walk, and the blind to see: and they glorified the God of Israel. —Matt. xv. 30, 31.

The power of healing was transmitted by our Lord to others. He not only gave the first company of disciples power to heal, but He authorised them to raise the dead. The first band of disciples who were commanded to preach the Gospel of the kingdom numbered twelve, and to these He gave power to work miracles.

And when He had called unto Him His twelve disciples He gave them power against unclean spirits, to cast them out, and to heal all manner of sickness and all manner of disease.

These twelve Jesus sent forth, and commanded them, saying, Go not into the way of the Gentiles, and into any city of the Samaritans enter ye not :

But go rather to the lost sheep of the house of Israel,

> And as ye go, preach, saying,
> The kingdom of heaven is at hand.
> Heal the sick, cleanse the lepers,
> raise the dead, cast out devils: freely
> ye have received, freely give.—Matt.
> x. 1, 5-8.

A little later He appointed another seventy and these too were commissioned and given power to heal the sick.

> After these things the Lord ap-
> pointed other seventy also, and sent
> them two and two before His face
> into every city and place, whither He
> Himself would come.
> Therefore said He unto them, The
> harvest truly is great, but the
> labourers are few: pray ye therefore
> the Lord of the harvest, that He
> would send forth labourers into His
> harvest.
> And into whatsoever city ye enter,
> and they receive you, eat such things
> as are set before you:
> And heal the sick that are therein,
> and say unto them, The kingdom of
> God is come nigh unto you.—Luke
> x. 1, 2, 8, 9.

PURPOSE OF MIRACLES AND HEALINGS.

It is evident to the careful reader of the Gospels that miracles and healings served more than one purpose. They were not only given to attest the ministry of our Lord and those He had appointed, but they were instrumental in attracting people to Christ and in encouraging

faith. Let us take some instances in the Gospel
of John. In chapter ii., verse 11, we read,
" This beginning of miracles did Jesus in Cana
of Galilee, and manifested forth His glory ; and
His disciples believed on Him." In verse 23
of the same chapter we read, " Now when He
was in Jerusalem at the passover, in the feast
day, many believed in His Name, when they
saw the miracles which He did." Nicodemus
in chapter iii., referred to our Lord's miracles,
and the inference is that they were partly the
means of bringing him to Christ. In chapter
vi., verse 2, we are told, " And a great multitude followed Him, because they saw His
miracles which He did on them that were
diseased." It was the miracle of the loaves
and fishes that drew forth the following testimony from those who stood near, " This is of
a truth that prophet that should come into the
world." It was the miracles that made people
conclude that Jesus was the Christ, for
they said, in chapter vii., verse 31, " When
Christ cometh, will He do more miracles than
these which this Man hath done ? " In chapter xi., verse 45, we read of many Jews believing, after seeing the things which Jesus
did. It was the miracle of the raising of
Lazarus from the dead that made the Jews
of chapter xii., verse 11, believe on Jesus, and
again it was the miracle that brought more
people into contact with Him according to the
18th verse.

CHAPTER VIII

Bodily Healing in the Dispensation of the Holy Ghost

*But this is that which was spoken by the prophet Joel:
And it shall come to pass in the last days, saith God,
I will pour out of My Spirit upon all flesh . . .*
—Acts ii. 16, 17.

*. . . Grant unto Thy servants, that with all boldness
they may speak Thy Word, by stretching forth Thine
hand to heal; and that signs and wonders may be
done by the Name of Thy holy Child Jesus.—*
Acts iv. 29, 30.

MOST Bible students agree concerning the commencement and continuation of this most remarkable dispensation. It was ushered in by a great and glorious demonstration of the supernatural, and it is destined to pass out with a still greater and more glorious manifestation of the power of God. Prophets and seers had long foretold the day when Pentecost, the second of the three great yearly and typical feasts of Jehovah, would merge into its antitype. Saints of God, still clothed with the Spirit of prophecy, are looking forward to another day, when the same dispensation will wind up with the translation of all regenerated ones in an ecstasy of praise. The Book of Acts opens with the scene of a company of faithful disciples, all full of joyous anticipation, preparing themselves for a new experience. The ten days' prayer convention in which they participated was soon over, and a dispensation more astonishing in its supernatural characteristics than any previous broke in upon them. The room of prayer and waiting had become one of praise and realisation, until it was filled with the sound of the rushing mighty Wind, that was present to inaugurate the long-looked-for dispensation. These disciples had evidently read of the God of the miraculous, who in the past occasionally came out of His palace and manifested His glory. They had heard of His signs in Egypt, of the crossing of the Red Sea, of His miracles in the wilderness, of the giving of the law on Sinai, of the fire-cloud that shone in the desert; and of the wonders which occupied so much room in the Scriptures they treasured. They had also lived in the dispensation of the Son, right in the company of Jesus, and had seen His miracles. He had walked the foaming billows, and stilled the fury of the tempest. He had prayed a few loaves into a mountain of bread, and had multiplied a few fish until there was sufficient for thousands. He had opened the eyes of the blind, restored the paralysed limb, and had raised the dead to life. They had also been eye-witnesses of His greater miracles. They were at the Cross when the earth shook, when the graves opened, when the rocks were rent, and when nature clothed itself in mourning. They had known the power of His resurrection in the rolling away of the stone, the breaking of the Roman seal, His coming forth from the dead, and His wonderful interviews so lovingly granted them during the forty days' period. They had witnessed the miracle of His ascension when the cloud received Him up out of their sight. There could be no question of their not being acquainted with the supernatural, for they had lived and moved in a world of miracles. Yet on this day they experienced workings in the supernatural that had never been known before. It pleased God to introduce new features into the dispensation of the Holy Ghost that were not to be found in the others. Physical signs and manifestations of a new order were this day bestowed upon them all. Jehovah was evidently emphasising the supernatural aspect of the new dispensation that was being ushered in. We have considered the truth of bodily healing in the dispensation of the Father, according to the Old Testament. We have also dealt with the subject of bodily healing in the dispensation of the Son, according to the Gospels. We shall now consider the subject in the dispensation of the Holy Ghost, according to the Acts of the Apostles and the Epistles. At this juncture it would be well for us to enquire if our Lord gave any commands or left any instructions concerning the healing of the sick in this dispensation. Yes, He did;

and these were included in what was almost the last message He gave before He ascended to His Father's throne.

SCOPE AND CREDENTIALS FOR HOLY GHOST MINISTRY.

> And He said unto them, Go ye into all the world, and preach the Gospel to every creature.
>
> He that believeth and is baptised shall be saved; but he that believeth not shall be damned.
>
> And these signs shall follow them that believe; In My Name shall they cast out devils; they shall speak with new tongues;
>
> They shall take up serpents; and if they drink any deadly thing it shall not hurt them; they shall lay hands on the sick, and they shall recover.
>
> So then after the Lord had spoken unto them, He was received up into heaven, and sat on the right hand of God.
>
> And they went forth and preached everywhere, the Lord working with them, and confirming the Word with signs following.—Mark xvi. 15-20.

We now come to the first healing miracle that is recorded after Pentecost. A lame man lying at the gate of the Temple is suddenly healed in the Name of the Lord. He had been a cripple from birth, and had been carried by friends day after day to the entrance of the Temple, to enable him to find a living by asking alms. It was to this poor man, over whose head forty summers had passed, that the great touch of Divine healing came in the dispensation of the Holy Ghost.

FIRST HEALING MIRACLE.

And a certain man lame from his mother's womb was carried, whom they laid daily at the gate of the temple which is called Beautiful, to ask alms of them that entered into the temple;

Who seeing Peter and John about to go into the temple asked an alms.

And Peter, fastening his eyes upon him with John, said, Look on us.

And he gave heed unto them, expecting to receive something of them.

Then Peter said, Silver and gold have I none; but such as I have give I thee: In the Name of Jesus Christ of Nazareth rise up and walk.

And he took him by the right hand, and lifted him up: and immediately his feet and ankle bones received strength.

And he leaping up stood, and walked, and entered with them into the temple, walking, and leaping, and praising God.—Acts iii. 2-8.

Soon after the healing of the lame man, the Name that had brought him deliverance was assailed, and the Apostles themselves were persecuted. Those who were stirred up against them were not slow to perceive the result that such healings would have upon the people. Something would have to be done to hinder this thing, or everyone would leave the long and well-established form of religion, and they would come to naught. These pioneers of a new sect must be silenced at all costs. So Peter and John were brought to the council, and examined by that august assembly. They produce their authority, and give the Name of the One responsible for the deed. Jesus of Nazareth who was crucified had been raised from the dead ; He was alive, and through His Name this man was made whole.

THE POWER OF HIS NAME.

Then Peter, filled with the Holy Ghost, said unto them, Ye rulers of the people, and elders of Israel,

If we this day be examined of the good deed done to the impotent man, by what means he is made whole;

Be it known unto you all, and to all the people of Israel, that by the Name of Jesus Christ of Nazareth, whom ye crucified, whom God raised from the dead, even by Him doth this man stand here before you whole.— Acts iv. 8-10.

PRAYERS FOR HEALING IN THE EARLY CHURCH ANSWERED.

By stretching forth thine hand to heal; and that signs and wonders may be done by the Name of Thy holy Child Jesus.—Acts iv. 30 (see also verses 12, 15, 16).

SAUL HEALED OF BLINDNESS.

And he was three days without sight, and neither did eat nor drink.

And Ananias went his way, and entered into the house; and putting his hands on him said, Brother Saul, the Lord, even Jesus, that appeared unto thee in the way as thou camest, hath sent me, that thou mightest receive thy sight, and be filled with the Holy Ghost.

And immediately there fell from his eyes as it had been scales; and he received sight forthwith, and arose, and was baptised.—Acts ix. 9, 17, 18.

HEALINGS IN SAMARIA.

Then Philip went down to the city of Samaria, and preached Christ unto them.

And the people with one accord gave heed unto those things which Philip spake, hearing and seeing the miracles which he did.

For unclean spirits, crying with loud voice, came out of many that were possessed with them: and many taken with palsies, and that were lame, were healed.

And there was great joy in that city.—Acts viii. 5-8.

HELPLESS MAN HEALED AT LYDDA.

And it came to pass, as Peter passed throughout all quarters, he came down also to the saints which dwelt at Lydda.

And there he found a certain man named Æneas, which had kept his bed eight years, and was sick of the palsy.

And Peter said unto him, Æneas, Jesus Christ maketh thee whole: arise, and make thy bed. And he arose immediately.

And all that dwelt at Lydda and Saron saw him, and turned to the Lord.—Acts ix. 32-35.

A CRIPPLE HEALED AT LYSTRA.

And there sat a certain man at Lystra, impotent in his feet, being a cripple from his mother's womb, who never had walked:

The same heard Paul speak: who stedfastly beholding him, and perceiving that he had faith to be healed,

Said with a loud voice, Stand upright on thy feet. And he leaped and walked.—Acts xiv. 8-10.

A DEMON-POSSESSED WOMAN HEALED.

And it came to pass, as we went to prayer, a certain damsel possessed with a spirit of divination met us, which brought her masters much gain by soothsaying:

The same followed Paul and us, and cried, saying, These men are the servants of the most high God, which shew unto us the way of salvation.

And this did she many days. But Paul, being grieved, turned and said to the spirit, I command thee in the

Name of Jesus Christ to come out of her. And he came out the same hour.—Acts xvi. 16-18.

IMMUNITY FROM VIPER'S POISONOUS BITE.

And when Paul had gathered a bundle of sticks, and laid them on the fire, there came a viper out of the heat, and fastened on his hand.

And when the barbarians saw the venomous beast hang on his hand, they said among themselves, No doubt this man is a murderer, whom, though he hath escaped the sea, yet vengeance suffereth not to live.

And he shook off the beast into the fire, and felt no harm.

Howbeit they looked when he should have swollen, or fallen down dead suddenly : but after they had looked a great while, and saw no harm come to him, they changed their minds, and said that he was a god. —Acts xxviii. 3-6.

ISLAND CHIEF'S FATHER HEALED OF FEVER.

And it came to pass, that the father of Publius lay sick of a fever and of a bloody flux : to whom Paul entered in, and prayed, and laid his hands on him, and healed him.— Acts xxviii. 8.

OTHER DISEASES HEALED ON THE ISLE OF MELITA.

So when this was done, others also which had diseases in the island, came, and were healed :

Who also honoured us with many honours; and when we departed, they laded us with such things as were necessary.—Acts xxviii. 9, 10.

GIFTS OF HEALINGS AMONG THE MIRACULOUS GIFTS.

But the manifestation of the Spirit is given to every man to profit withal.

For to one is given by the Spirit the word of wisdom; to another the word of knowledge by the same Spirit;

To another faith by the same Spirit; to another the gifts of healing by the same Spirit;

To another the working of miracles; to another prophecy; to another discerning of spirits; to another divers kinds of tongues; to another the interpretation of tongues:

But all these worketh that one and the selfsame Spirit, dividing to every man severally as He will.—I. Cor. xii. 7-11.

GIFTS OF HEALINGS IN THE CHURCH UNIVERSAL.

Now ye are the body of Christ, and members in particular.

And God hath set some in the church, first apostles, secondarily prophets, thirdly teachers, after that miracles, then gifts of healings, helps, governments, diversities of tongues.—I. Cor. xii. 27, 28.

HEALING IN THE EPISTLE OF JAMES.

> Is any sick among you? let him call for the elders of the church; and let them pray over him, anointing him with oil in the Name of the Lord:
>
> And the prayer of faith shall save the sick, and the Lord shall raise him up; and if he have committed sins, they shall be forgiven him.—James v. 14, 15.

Having followed the course of bodily healing throughout the whole of Scripture, we now reach the stage where the last inspired word added to Scripture made the book one complete whole. It is unnecessary to explain what is obvious to every reader of the New Testament, that the dispensation of the Holy Ghost did not end when the canon of Scripture closed. But it is most necessary to emphasize that it has not changed one whit from its essential and supernatural character, and that it cannot change until the coming of Christ. God's inspired Word, complete and perfectly whole, was the chart given to guide the Church through future centuries, the compass to direct it on the sea of life. The revelation of the Divine mind, given in full upon the printed page, was sealed, and nothing could be added or taken away. But the dispensation continued on its course, and will continue until the return of Christ. Henceforth the only true position for every soul that should be regenerated, and every church that should be established, was to stand foursquare for the doctrines it contained, teaching only what it taught, and making it the final court of authority in every question.

> All Scripture is given by inspiration of God, and is profitable for doctrine, for reproof, for correction, for instruction in righteousness:
>
> That the man of God may be perfect, throughly furnished unto all good works.—II. Tim, iii. 16, 17.

CHAPTER IX

The Canon of Scripture Closed:
the Dispensation of the Holy Ghost Continues

Go ye into all the world, and preach the gospel to every creature.—Mark xvi. 15.

Teaching them to observe all things whatsoever I have commanded you: and lo, I am with you alway, even unto the end of the world.—Matt. xxviii. 20.

IT is almost 2,000 years since the sacred canon of scripture was closed, but the dispensation of the Holy Ghost, with its miracles, signs and wonders, continues to this present day. Believers of the twentieth century, with those of the first, live in the same dispensation. The gospel message that brought men and women to Christ in the days of the Apostles is still converting sinners. The Holy Spirit who convicted then is still convicting and converting to-day. Yet some Bible students are in the unenviable position of trying to reconcile the experience of regeneration with the view that the days of miracles have ceased. It is most difficult sometimes to arouse them to the astounding claims of the religion they have embraced. They have a vague idea that Christianity is only to be experienced in the intellect, and all that it claims from them is mere assent to certain truths and doctrines.

Christianity and the miraculous are, to their minds, terms that are diametrical opposites. To suggest that they are in any way related or linked together is to become visionary, fanatical, and extreme in views. The very idea of anyone laying claim to the gifts of healing or of working of miracles seems to be bordering on heresy. How this position can be maintained in the light of the supernatural element in Christianity is most difficult to understand, for the Christian religion is essentially a religion of the miraculous. The definition of the term *miracle* is " a supernatural effect or event." Christianity without such effects is a contradiction in terms. The supernatural has been woven into the whole fabric of the Christian faith. Thus there are :

The miraculous Virgin Birth.

The miraculous life of Christ.

The miraculous prodigies attending the Cross.

The miraculous Resurrection.

The miraculous Ascension.

The miraculous outpouring of the Holy Ghost.

The miraculous Second Advent.

Belief in the above cardinal and fundamental truths certainly implies faith in the supernatural. Then, again, the attitude of the person who believes in conversion, in prayer, and in the Bible itself, is not consistent with the claim that the days of miracles are past, for these are miracles in themselves.

REGENERATION IS A MIRACLE.

Every real conversion to Christ means the working of a miracle. Some change takes place in the experience of the true convert that can only be wrought through the Divine agency of the supernatural. This change the Scripture calls a new birth, or a passing from death into life. To be born again is to become a partaker of Divine nature, and to pass from death into life means the beginning of a life never before experienced. It is impossible for a person to become a partaker of Divine nature, and for spiritual life to begin in the soul of one dead in sins, apart from the miraculous.

PRAYER IS A MIRACLE.

Millions pray at the same time ; many and varied are the petitions that are laid before the Throne ; and all expect to be heard by the one God. The attitude of every praying Christian is a testimony of faith in the miraculous.

THE BIBLE A MIRACLE.

This " grand old Book," which is a lamp unto our feet and a light unto our path, is nothing less than a miracle. Its sixty-six books, the compilation of over thirty writers, took over fifteen hundred years to complete. Persons in the varied callings and stations of life were used to put it together—kings and shepherds, scholars and fishermen, priests and politicians, a doctor and a tax-collector. The first man to write had gone the way of all flesh long before the last began ; yet from the first verse in Genesis to the last verse in Revelation, there is not one single contradiction. You may search in vain to find inaccuracies, because they are only supposed. The one Divine Author, moving each of its writers, has given us a complete Bible that will stand the tests of all time. Again, the way in which the Bible has been preserved is truly miraculous. In defiance of all the terrible onslaughts of the enemy, and of all the fires that have been kindled for its destruction, it remains indestructible. Voltaire predicted the extinction of the Bible within a hundred years of his day, but it still lives on, while he is dead and gone ; the house in which he lived is now a Bible house, containing thousands of copies of the miracle Book.

THE MIRACULOUS SIGNS.

The command and promises of Mark xvi. 15-18 most certainly apply to the whole dispensation of the Holy Ghost.

There was no geographical boundary to limit its activities—'' Go ye into all the world.''

There was no distinction of class to hinder its message—" Preach the Gospel to every creature."

There was no cessation of the miraculous signs—" These signs shall follow them that believe."

There was no change in the authority behind the commission—" In My Name."

HEALINGS AFTER THE CANON OF SCRIPTURE WAS CLOSED.

Nevertheless He left not Himself without witness.—Acts xiv. 17.

Church records and memoirs of the early Christians, combined with what we have personally experienced and seen with our own eyes, furnish the evidence to prove that miracles of healing abound in this continued dispensation. The Rev. A. J. Gordon, D.D., of Boston, the well-known theologian and preacher, who was undoubtedly a scholarly saint as well as a saintly scholar, has carefully culled from the writings of the early saints references to miracles of healing. Dr. Gordon himself was a firm believer in Divine healing, and he has presented to the world his excellent book, *The Ministry of Healing*. In it he clearly proves that miracles of bodily healing, however much they have at times decreased, have never entirely ceased. We are indebted to this revered servant of Christ for the following testimonies which have been selected from the splendid and indisputable mass of evidence contained in *The Ministry of Healing*—Justin Martyr, Irenæus, Tertullian, Origen, Clement, Dr. Waterland, Dodwell, Dr. Marshall, the Waldenses, the Moravians, Zinzendorf, the Hugenots and Luther.

THE TESTIMONY OF JUSTIN MARTYR.

" For numberless demoniacs throughout the whole world and in your city, many of our Christian men, exorcising them in the name of Jesus Christ, who was crucified under Pontius Pilate, have healed, and do heal, rendering helpless and driving the possessing devils out of the men, though they could not be cured by all the other exorcists and those who used incantations and drugs."

THE TESTIMONY OF IRENÆUS.

" Wherefore also those who are in truth the disciples, receiving grace from Him, do in His name perform miracles, so as to promote the welfare of others, according to the gift which each has received from Him. . . . Others still heal the sick by laying their hands upon them, and they are made whole."

THE TESTIMONY OF TERTULLIAN.

" For the clerk of one of them, who was liable to be thrown upon the ground by an evil spirit, was set free from his affliction, as was also the relative of another, and the little boy of a third. And how many men of rank, to say nothing of the common people, have been delivered from devils and healed of disease."

THE TESTIMONY OF ORIGEN.

" And some give evidence of their having received through their faith a marvellous power by the cures which they perform, invoking no other name over those who need their help than that of the God of all things and of Jesus, along with a mention of His history. For by these means we too have seen many persons freed from grievous calamities and from distractions of mind and madness, and countless other ills which could be cured neither by men nor devils."

THE TESTIMONY OF CLEMENT.

Giving directions for visiting the sick and afflicted—" Let them, therefore, with fasting and prayer, make their intercessions, and not with the well-arranged and fitly ordered words of learning, but as men who have received the gift of healing confidently, to the glory of God."

Dr. Gordon writes : " The weight of these and like testimonies is so generally acknowledged by Church historians that it seems little less than hardihood for scholars to go on repeating that well-worn phrase, ' The age of miracles ended with the apostles.' "

117

He then refers to the declarations of the following :

Dr. Waterland : "The miraculous gifts continued through the third century, at least."

Dodwell : " Though they generally ceased with the third century, there are several strongly attested cases in the fourth."

Dr. Marshall, the translator of Cyprian : "There are successive evidences of them down to the age of Constantine."

How true it is that when the Church compromises with the world and diverts from the pathway of holiness, the power of God is withdrawn. It has been so from the beginning. The Creator withdrew from the first man because of transgression, the glory of God was withdrawn from the Temple in the land because of the backsliding of the people. To-day the community or church that mixes with the world, and does not stand for separation from it, need not expect an outpouring of the Holy Ghost. It is easy to understand why the supernatural decreased at the time of Constantine, for it was an age of worldly compromise on the part of the Christian Church. Dr. Gordon says, " The age of Constantine is a significant date at which to fix the termination of miracles. For almost all Church historians hold that there was a period when the simpler and purer forms of supernatural manifestation ceased to be generally recognized, or were supplanted by the gross and spurious type which characterize the Church of the middle ages. And the era of Constantine's conversion confessedly marks a decided transition from a purer to a more degenerate and worldly Christianity. From this period on, we find the Church ceasing to depend wholly on the Lord in heaven, and to rest in the patronage and support of earthly rulers ; and ceasing to look ever for the coming and Kingdom of Christ as the consummation of her hopes, and to exult in her present triumph and worldly splendour. But now comes a most suggestive fact ; that, whenever we find a revival of primitive faith and apostolic simplicity, there we find a profession of the chaste and evangelical miracles which characterized the apostolic age. These attend the cradle of every spiritual reformation, as they did the birth of the Church herself. Waldenses, Moravians, Huguenots, Covenanters, Friends, Baptists, and Methodists all have their record of them."

THE TESTIMONY OF THE WALDENSES.

" Therefore, concerning this anointing of the sick, we hold it as an article of faith, and profess sincerely from the heart that sick persons, when they ask it, may lawfully be anointed with the anointing oil by one who joins with them in praying that it may be efficacious to the healing of the body, according to the design and end and effect mentioned by the apostles ; and we profess that such an anointing, performed according to the apostolic design and practice, will be healing and profitable."

THE TESTIMONY OF THE MORAVIANS.

" We are, indeed, well aware that, so far from its being possible to prove by Scripture, or by experience, that visions and dreams, the gift of miracles, healings and extraordinary gifts, have absolutely ceased in Christendom since the apostolic times, it is on the contrary proved, both by facts and by scripture, that there may always be these gifts where there is faith, and that they will never be entirely detached from it. We need only take care to discern the true from the false, and to distinguish miracles proceeding from the Holy Ghost from lying miracles, or those which without being so decidedly of the Devil do not so decidedly indicate the presence of the Lord."

THE TESTIMONY OF ZINZENDORF.

" To believe against hope is the root of the gift of miracles ; and I owe this testimony to our beloved Church, that apostolic powers are there manifested. We have had undeniable proofs thereof in the unequivocal discovery of things, persons, and circumstances, which could not humanly have been discovered, in the healing of maladies in themselves incurable, such as cancers, consumptions, when the patient was in the agonies of death, etc., all by means of prayer, or of a single word."

THE TESTIMONY OF THE HUGUENOTS.

" If we come to the Huguenots, those faithful followers of the Lamb, among generations that were so greedily and wantonly following the Dragon, we get glimpses of the same wonderful things. In the story of their suffering and obedience to the faith in the mountains of the Cevennes, whither they had fled from their pursuers upon the revocation of the Edict of Nantes, we hear constant mention of the exercise of miraculous gifts. There were Divine healings, and extraordinary actings of the Spirit in quickening and inspiration. They who in their exile carried their mechanical arts and inventions into England, to the great blessing of the nation, carried here and there the lost arts of supernatural healing to the wonder of the Church of Christ."

THE TESTIMONY OF MARTIN LUTHER.

" How often has it happened, and still does, that devils have been driven out in the name of Christ; also, by calling on His name and prayer, that the sick have been healed."

CHAPTER X

Dispensation of the Holy Ghost Continues : Miracles and Healings

Ye are My witnesses.—Isaiah xliii. 10.

THE SCOTTISH COVENANTERS.

IT is impossible to read the thrilling records of these noble sons of Scotland, given by the saintly John Howie in *Scots Worthies,* without being inspired in the Christian faith. We shall never forget how, when ministering in the land of the Covenanters for the first time, our hearts were warmed as we perused its soul-stirring pages. The names of Wishart, Knox, Welch, Livingstone, Craig, and Peden, on the roll of honour in the preface bring to remembrance impassioned prayers, noble deeds, enduring trials, and triumphant faith. Their lives have been held aloft in Christian pulpits as examples of holy living, their heroic faith and passion for souls as blessings to be coveted. These illustrious saints believed in the God of the supernatural, and it is not surprising to know that Divine interposition frequently attended their ministries. Yet preachers have been strangely silent on the miraculous aspect of their ministry. Is it because they have considered such startling answers to prayer impossible in modern times? The following miracle, as a result of the importunate prayer of Welch, is recorded in this remarkable book, page 293 :

" There was in his house, amongst many others who boarded with him for good education, a young gentleman of great quality, and suitable expectations, the heir of Lord Ochiltree, captain of the castle of Edinburgh. This young nobleman, after he had gained very much upon Welch's affections, fell ill of a grievous sickness, and after he had been long wasted with it, he, to the apprehension of all spectators, closed his eyes and expired. He was therefore taken out of his bed, and laid on a pallet on the floor, that his body might be more conveniently dressed. This was to Welch a great grief, and therefore he stayed with the dead body full three hours, lamenting over him with great tenderness. After twelve hours, the friends brought in a coffin, and desired the corpse might be put into it, as the custom was ; but Welch requested that, for his satisfaction, they would forbear it for a time. This was granted, and they did not return till twenty-four hours after his death. They then desired, with great importunity, that the corpse might be coffined and speedily buried, the weather being extremely hot. The good man still persisted, however, in his request, and earnestly begged them to excuse him once more ; so they left the corpse upon the pallet

123

for full thirty-six hours : but even after that, as he urged not only with great earnestness, but with some displeasure, they were constrained to forbear for twelve hours more. After forty-eight hours were past, he still held out against them ; and then his friends, perceiving that he believed the young man was not really dead, but under some fit, proposed to him, for satisfaction, that trial should be made upon his body, if possibly any spark of life might be found in him ; to which he agreed. The doctors accordingly were set to work ; they pinched him in the fleshy parts of his body, and twisted a bow-string about his head with great force ; but no sign of life appearing, they pronounced him dead, and then there was no more delay to be made. Yet Welch begged of them once more that they would but step into the next room for an hour or two, and leave him with the dead youth ; and this they granted. He then fell down before the pallet, and cried to the Lord, with all his might, and sometimes looking upon the dead body, he continued to wrestle with the Lord, till at length the youth opened his eyes, and cried out to Welch, whom he distinctly knew, ' O sir, I am whole, but my head and legs ! ' These were the places hurt with the pinching. When Welch perceived this, he called his friends, and shewed them the dead man restored to life again, to their great astonishment. This young nobleman, though he lost the estate of

Ochiltree, lived to inherit one not inferior in Ireland, became Lord Castlestuart, and was a man of such excellent parts, that he was courted by the Earl of Stafford to be a councillor in Ireland . . . This story the nobleman himself communicated to his friends in Ireland.''

That Howie, the author of *Scots Worthies,* anticipated a cold reception on the part of some of his readers for the records he was preparing is evident from the remarks in the preface, page 12 :

'' Some may be ready,'' he says, '' to object that many things related in this collection smell too much of enthusiasm ; and that other things narrated therein are beyond all credit. But these we must suppose to be either quite ignorant of what the Lord did for our forefathers in former times, or else, in a great measure, destitute of the like gracious influences of the Holy Spirit by which they were actuated and animated.''

For his arduous labour in collating the deeds and miracles of those faithful servants of Christ he quite expected from the carnal-minded the rebuff of being over-enthusiastic. There is a similarity in the method of attack made on the operations of the Holy Spirit by unbelieving opposers in every age. In his day, like ours, the manifestation of the Spirit, in the ministry even of the choicest saints, was considered to be mere enthusiasm, and any testimony to miracles and healings as given by a visionary. The raising of the dead is certainly an extraordinary happening, and it must be clearly understood that it is most exceptional in the present dispensation. The raising of the dead is not included in the signs that were to follow them that believe (Mark xvi. 15-18).

THE TESTIMONY OF JOHN WESLEY.

It is well to remind the conservative element in the Christian Church of to-day who regard anything in the nature of miraculous healing as unorthodox, that no less a person than the great founder of Methodism believed in Divine healing . In his *Notes on the New Testament* he records his views on James v. 14 thus : " This single conspicuous gift which Christ committed to His apostles remained in the Church long after the miraculous gifts. Indeed, it seems to have been designed to remain always, and St. James directs the elders, who were the most if not the only gifted men, to administer it. This was the whole process of physics in the Church till it was lost through unbelief." In his Journal he gives his own testimony of healing. ' When I was about seven and twenty, I began spitting blood, and continued for several years. Eleven years after, I was in the third stage of consumption ; it pleased God in three months to remove this also. This hath God wrought.' "

THE TESTIMONY OF GEORGE FOX.

There are many miracles of healing recorded in the Journal of this honoured servant of God. We have already referred to his own remarkable testimony in the chapter on the Mortal Body. The following instantaneous healing is given on page 219 :

" After some time I went to a meeting at Arn-Side, where Richard Myer was, who had been long lame of one of his arms. I was moved of the Lord to say unto him, amongst all the people, ' Stand up upon thy legs ' (for he was sitting down) : and he stood up, and stretched out his arm that had been lame a long time, and said, ' Be it known unto you, all people, that this day I am healed.' Yet his parents could hardly believe it ; but after the meeting was done, they had him aside, took off his doublet, and then saw it was true. He came soon after to Swarthmore meeting, and then declared how that the Lord had healed him.''

THE TESTIMONY OF J. N. DARBY.

In childlike faith this beloved pioneer among the Brethren stepped out on the promises of God to heal, as the following extract shews. It is taken from an appendix to *By What Means?* by Philip Mauro. It is clear that J. N. Darby, who knew the Word of God as few have ever known it, believed that Divine healing for the body was one of the present benefits of the last Adam's obedience. " An old Brother, who had served Christ in the ministry of the Word for over fifty years, and who knew Mr. Darby and other teachers personally and well, writes, under date of August 10, 1910, as follows :

" ' I have letters from Mr. Darby, stating that prayers for the sick, and healing as the result of the prayer of faith, were common among Brethren at the beginning. In the great cholera plague of 1832 this was so effective that the doctors were in " consternation." But a physician, who was impressed with the results of the prayer of faith, asked for prayer for some of his patients ; " medicine was relinquished," and the patients recovered. When I was in Guernsey, in 1866, Mr. Carey, who has been in the South of France with Mr. Darby, told me of the son of a Congregational minister who had been almost instantly healed through the prayer of faith of Mr. Darby.' "

THE TESTIMONY OF DR. CULLIS.

The work of this renowned physician and philanthropist was a perfect example of healing in the two realms, supernatural and natural. The following description of his work in Boston, and also the case of healing under Dr. Cullis, is taken from Dr. Gordon's *Ministry of Healing* :

" Dr. Charles Cullis is at the head of what is known as the ' faith-work ' in the city of Boston. The work had many branches, the Consumptives' Home ; the Willard Tract Repository ; homes for children ; city mission work ; foreign missionary work ; schools among the freedmen, etc., all maintained upon the same principle virtually as the orphan work of Pastor George Muller, at Bristol in England. Anyone who has been made acquainted with a single department of this enterprise, as for example, that of the Consumptives' Home, can have no doubt as to the most beneficent and Christlike character of the labours carried on."

The following extract from *The Bible and the Body,* by Rowland V. Bingham, emphasising healing in the two realms, clearly shews the position we have consistently held during the seventeen years we have been privileged to stand for the truth. " Dr. Charles Cullis was a practising physician, of whom the profession might well be proud. He was really one of the advance guard to wage war on the modern scourge of mankind, tuberculosis. He was not only a physician, but a philanthropist, founding an institution where he could minister to many sick and suffering ones who would otherwise have been unable to afford the care which he gave. But, while he was a busy doctor, he was a diligent student of the Word of God, and a man of prayer. In his medical work he often came to the end of his own resources, and, like every honest physician, had to acknowledge that human aid and medical help had reached its limit. It was under these circumstances he was led to seek Divine assistance, and the answers to his prayers were many. A careful study of the Scriptures convinced him that there were promises which he could rightly plead on behalf of the sick. Especially did he make use of the promise and instruction in the fifth chapter of the Epistle of St. James. It was his custom to render what medical aid he could. Then he would seek to administer spiritual comfort or admonition from the Word. Where he perceived that they had faith to be healed, he was always ready to pray the prayer of faith. Many were those who were past all help from human sources who were restored in answer to prayer. But with Dr. Cullis there was no attempt to resolve these experiences of healing into a system of theology, nor did he ever see any incongruity between the use of his medical knowledge and seeking the Divine intervention. He did not presume to dictate to God as to which plane He would operate on, the natural or the supernatural. And yet, far from shewing Divine displeasure that this man continued to act as the beloved physician in all cases where natural healing was possible, God blessed this man's ministry in supernatural healing beyond almost any other instrument of our day—until the record of the cases restored to health would require volumes.''

PHYSICIAN PRAYS—TUMOUR DISAPPEARS.

The following remarkable case of healing given in Dr. Cullis's own words is taken from Dr. Gordon's *Ministry of Healing*. The renowned physician anointed one of his patients with oil according to James v., and in answer to his prayer she was healed of tumour.

'' I had under my professional care a Christian lady, with a tumour which confined her almost continuously to her bed in severe suffering. All remedies were unavailing, and the only human hope was the knife : but, feeling in my heart the power of the promise, I one morning sat down by her bedside, and taking up the Bible, I read aloud God's promise to His believing children : ' And the prayer of faith shall save the sick, and the Lord shall raise him up ; and if he have committed sins, they shall be forgiven him.' I then asked her if she would trust the Lord to remove this tumour and to restore her to health, and to her missionary work. She replied, ' I have no particular faith about it, but am willing to trust the Lord for it.' I then knelt and anointed her with oil in the Name of the Lord, asking Him to fulfil His own Word. Soon after I left, she got up and walked three miles. From that time the tumour rapidly lessened, until all trace of it at length disappeared.''

THE TESTIMONY OF DR. STANLEY JONES.

This world-famous missionary and author, whose writings are among the foremost of the present day, makes the following interesting confession concerning the teaching of Divine healing. It is taken from his book, *The Christ of Every Road.*

'' I have almost run away from physical healing through prayer, and yet again and again I have been all but forced into it.

In *The Christ of the Indian Road* he gives a personal experience of bodily healing.

'' I saw that unless I got help from somewhere I would have to give up my missionary career, go back to America, and go to work on a farm to try to regain my health. It was one of my darkest hours. At that time I was in a meeting at Lucknow. While in prayer, not particularly thinking about myself, a Voice seemed to say, ' Are you yourself ready for this work to which I have called you? ' I replied, ' No, Lord, I am done for. I have reached the end of my rope.' The Voice replied, ' If you will turn that over to Me, and not worry about it, I will take care of it.' I quickly answered, ' Lord, I close the bargain right here.' A great peace settled into my heart and pervaded me. I knew it was done! Life—abundant Life—had taken possession of me . . . For days after that I hardly knew I had a body. I went through the days, working all day and far into the night, and came down to bed-time wondering why in the world I should ever go to bed at all, for there was not the slightest trace of tiredness of any kind. I seemed possessed by Life and Peace and Rest —by Christ Himself . . . Nine of the most strenuous years of my life have gone by since then, the old trouble has never returned, and I have never had such health. I seemed to have tapped new life for body, mind, and spirit. Life was on a permanently higher level. And I have done nothing but take it."

THE TESTIMONY OF DR. A. B. SIMPSON.

The name of the founder of the Christian Missionary Alliance is revered because of his faithful service in the Kingdom of God, and by many who have been led into the truth of Divine healing. After being a sufferer for some years, he was led to dedicate his body to the Lord and to trust Him for healing. Instead of going to a premature grave, he was marvellously restored to health, and for over twenty-five years he laboured unceasingly to the amazement of those who looked on. Referring to the subject of Divine healing in the preface to his book, *The Gospel of Healing,* he writes :

"The importance of this subject, and the emphatic way in which God's Holy Spirit is pressing it upon the attention of His people, demands for it the most careful and thorough scriptural study. Effectual faith can only come through thorough conviction. In spite of the cold and conservative, and sometimes scornful unbelief of many, this doctrine is becoming one of the touchstones of character and spiritual life in all the churches of America, and revolutionising, by a deep, quiet, and Divine movement, the whole Christian life of thousands. It has a profound bearing upon the spiritual life. No one can truly receive it without being a holier and more useful Christian."

THE TESTIMONY OF DR. ANDREW MURRAY.

This reverend saint of Christ, who is said to have influenced a whole generation in a way few men have, was a firm believer in Divine healing. In the preface to his own work on the subject, he writes :

"This healing, granted to faith, has been the source of rich spiritual blessing to me. I have clearly seen that the Church possesses in Jesus, our Divine Healer, an inestimable treasure, which she does not yet know how to appreciate. I have been convinced anew of that which the Word of God teaches us in this matter, and of what the Lord expects of us ;

and I am sure that if Christians learned to realise practically the presence of the Lord that healeth, their spiritual life would thereby be developed and sanctified. I can therefore no longer keep silence, and I publish here a series of meditations, with the view of shewing according to the Word of God, that " the prayer of faith " (James v. 15) is the means appointed by God for the cure of the sick, that this truth is in perfect accord with Holy Scripture, and that the study of this truth is essential for every one who would see the Lord manifest His power and His glory in the midst of His children."

The following account of his own healing is taken from *Andrew Murray and his Message,* by Rev. W. M. Douglas, B.A. :

" When in England, he was led to consider afresh the whole question of Divine healing, a subject on which he had often thought since his student days. After much prayer and consideration, and after consultation with the widely-known Pastor Stockmayer, Mr. Murray decided to enter Bethshan, a home opened in London by Dr. Boardman for such suffering believers as wished to be instructed in Biblical teaching on disease and healing, in answer to the prayer of faith, as understood by these devoted servants of Christ. Here he remained for some weeks, and in the mercy of God left it, completely healed, so that never again was he troubled by any weakness of throat or voice. His throat, in dependence constantly upon the Lord for its use, in spite of the heavy strain imposed upon it, for the rest of his life retained its strength till the end, and his voice retained its clear, musical, penetrating quality.''

THE TESTIMONY OF REV. SAMUEL CHADWICK.

In his *Path of Prayer*, the Principal of Cliff College and Editor of *Joyful News* has with characteristic courage declared his convictions on the truth of Divine healing, as follows :

'' There is healing through the prayer of faith. The truth of this is confirmed by many witnesses who are both sane and saintly. There are those to whom is given the gift of healing, and they lay hands upon the sick and they recover. I myself have been healed through the prayer of faith.''

In the same chapter he testifies to a most astounding case of healing that occurred in a convention at which he was present.

'' The most remarkable example of Divine healing I have known took place at the Southport Convention. The Rev. W. H. Tindall was president of the convention, and the strain of much speaking had brought on a disease of the throat. For more than a year he had not spoken above a whisper, and even that was painful. The specialists gave no hope of recovery. At all the meetings he was a pathetic and silent figure. Prayer was offered for him continually. At the speakers' prayer-meeting on the Friday morning there was a remarkable intensity and unity of faith. No one could pray for anything but the recovery of Mr. Tindall's voice. Faith gathered courage, forgot impossibilities, and claimed the promise. Dr. Ebenezer E. Jenkins presided, and when the rest of us rose from our knees, Mr. Tindall remained kneeling. Dr. Jenkins said, " This is the most remarkable prayer-meeting I have ever known," and placing his hand on the president's head he declared, in the Name of the Lord, that we should hear Mr. Tindall speak in the tent before the convention closed. That night Mr. Tindall spoke in the tent for fifteen minutes, and was heard by twelve hundred people, and he preached without loss of voice to the end of his days. I was present, and saw and heard, and there are those still alive to confirm my testimony."

CHAPTER XI

Miracles and Healings in the Present Dispensation

Questions—Difficulties—Explanations—Instruction

WE have seen that sickness is included in the effects of the first Adam's disobedience, and also that healing is one of the present benefits of the last Adam's obedience. We quite appreciate the problems that surround the teaching of Divine healing, and our sympathy is extended to those who are wrestling with difficulties. We offer no apology for the fanaticism of those who are extreme in their views and extravagant in practice; such we decidedly condemn. The presentation of this delicate subject necessitates handling by careful workmen who can rightly divide the Word of truth. Physical healing is undoubtedly one of the precious truths that have been neglected by the Church of Christ, and its neglect has resulted in her members accepting counterfeit teaching. Gaps allowed in Christian truth are soon filled with error, and the lack of Holy Ghost power creates a want that is readily supplied by the enemy. Our purpose in this chapter is to deal with questions, difficulties, and explanations, and to offer instruction for the help of those who are enquiring into the truth of Divine healing.

Divine healing versus faith healing.

Question:

Is there such a thing as faith-healing apart from Christianity?

Answer:

Faith-healing might mean healing by faith in the power of mind over matter, suggestion, or auto-suggestion. People who are called faith-healers can hold these views and be decidedly anti-Christian.

Question:

What is the difference between this kind of faith-healing and Divine healing which you teach?

Answer:

We teach people to seek bodily healing as one of the immediate benefits of Christ's atoning and redeeming work on the cross. We believe in the fundamentals of the Christian faith, and accept the Bible in its entirety as the Word of God. It is not the effect of mind over matter, but the power of Christ over disease.

> And when they had set them in the midst, they asked, By what power, or by what name, have ye done this?—Acts iv. 7.

> Be it known unto you all, and to all the people of Israel, that by the Name of Jesus Christ of Nazareth, whom ye crucified, whom God raised from the dead, even by Him doth this man stand here before you whole.—Acts iv. 10.

Salvation of souls more important.

Question:

Why take so much time considering the needs of the mortal body? Surely the salvation of the soul is of far greater importance, and the time devoted to the teaching of bodily healing could be more properly spent in saving souls?

Answer:

Kindly read chapter v. on " The Marvellous Mortal Body."

God's will to heal.

Question:

We all believe that God can heal, for He is omnipotent, but how do you know it is His will to heal people in these days?

Answer:

The will of God regarding the healing of the body is revealed in scriptural promises to heal in every dispensation, including the present one,

> Confess your faults one to another, and pray one for another, that ye may be healed. The effectual fervent prayer of a righteous man availeth much.—James v. 16.

Suffering saints and the will of God.

Question:

Are we to presume that all saints suffering from bodily affliction are out of line with the will of God?

Answer:

There is no authority in Scripture for the view that every saint who is suffering from sickness and disease is out of line with the will of God. The most devoted saints, such as Paul, Timothy, and Epaphroditus, suffered in body, but were certainly not out of God's will. The reason why God sometimes allows His saints to suffer is that they may be schooled and disciplined in the things pertaining to the kingdom of God.

> For whom the Lord loveth He chasteneth . . ,—Heb. xii. 6.
> And lest I should be exalted above measure through the abundance of the revelations, there was given to me a thorn in the flesh, the messenger of Satan to buffet me, lest I should be exalted above measure.——II. Cor. xii. 7.

141

Behold, we count them happy which
endure. Ye have heard of the
patience of Job, and have seen the
end of the Lord; that the Lord is
very pitiful, and of tender mercy.—
James v. 11.

Miracles not for this enlightened age.

Question:

Why advocate signs and miracles in confirmation of the Gospel message in this enlightened Christian age?

Answer:

If this is an enlightened Christian age it is strange that its battlefields have staged the greatest war ever known, drunk in the blood of millions of men, and caused additional millions of men, women and children to die of disease, pestilence, and famine. Since the Armistice thousands of pounds have been spent in celebrating peace. Peace ambassadors have sailed the seven seas, and countless peace conferences have been held. Yet as we write we have before us staggering figures shewing what sums are now being spent preparing for another war. An age that spends fifteen hundred pounds a minute on armaments alone does not sound like one that has been converted to Christ. This is an age of materialism, apostasy, and declension, and if miraculous signs were needed to confirm the Gospel message

142

nineteen hundred years ago, they are surely needed in these last days in a world that has drifted and is drifting away from God.

But of the times and the seasons, brethren, ye have no need that I write unto you.

For yourselves know perfectly that the day of the Lord so cometh as a thief in the night.

For when they shall say, Peace and safety; then sudden destruction cometh upon them, as travail upon a woman with child; and they shall not escape.—I. Thess. v. 1-3.

Now the Spirit speaketh expressly, that in the latter times some shall depart from the faith, giving heed to seducing spirits, and doctrines of devils.—I. Tim. iv, 1.

This know also, that in the last days perilous times shall come.

For men shall be lovers of their own selves, covetous, boasters, proud, blasphemers, disobedient to parents, unthankful, unholy,

Without natural affection, truce-breakers, false accusers, incontinent, fierce, despisers of those that are good,

Traitors, heady, highminded, lovers of pleasures more than lovers of God;

Having a form of godliness, but denying the power thereof: from such turn away.—II. Tim. iii. 1-5.

For nation shall rise against nation, and kingdom against kingdom : and

there shall be famines, and pesti-
lences, and earthquakes, in divers
places.—Matt. xxiv. 7.

Miracles and signs not withdrawn.

Question:

Is it not correct that miracles and signs were withdrawn at the close of the apostolic age?

Answer:

There is not a single verse in the whole of the Bible to shew that these miraculous gifts have been withdrawn at any time. On the contrary the Scripture clearly shews that these gifts, including healing, belong to the Church; and the Church, which comprises all the regenerated, is still on earth.

> Now ye are the body of Christ, and members in particular.
> And God hath set some in the church, first apostles, secondarily prophets, thirdly teachers, after that miracles, then gifts of healings, helps, governments, diversities of tongues.—I. Cor. xii. 27, 28.

Healing power withdrawn from Paul?

Question:

If the power to heal had not been withdrawn at the end of the apostolic days, why did Paul on one of his journeys allow a fellow-worker to remain sick at Miletum?

Answer:

The fact that Paul allowed Trophimus to remain sick at Miletum is no proof that the power to heal was withdrawn from the apostle. We read of our Lord healing some folk, whilst others were evidently not healed. Only one seemed to have been healed out of the great multitude that gathered at the Pool of Bethesda. Surely we are not to suppose that the power to heal had been withdrawn from our precious Lord.

Now there is at Jerusalem by the sheep market a pool, which is called in the Hebrew tongue Bethesda, having five porches.

In these lay a great multitude of impotent folk, of blind, halt, withered, waiting for the moving of the water.

And a certain man was there which had an infirmity thirty and eight years. When Jesus saw him lie, and knew that he had been now a long time in that case, He said unto him, Wilt thou be made whole?

The impotent man answered Him, Sir, I have no man, when the water is troubled, to put me into the pool, but while I am coming, another steppeth down before me.

Jesus saith unto him, Rise, take up thy bed and walk.

And immediately the man was made whole, and took up his bed and walked : and on the same day was the sabbath.—John v. 2, 3, 5-9.

Healing Rays

No miracles recorded after Acts xxviii.

Question:

Are people justified in saying that as there is no record of miracles and healings after Acts xxviii., they must have ceased at that time?

Answer:

Our readers will pardon the inclusion of this question, for its absurdity is obvious to all. Yet the line of argument it takes has been offered by some who have opposed the truth of bodily healing in our day. Surely there could be no further record of miracles and healings because the twenty-eighth chapter is the last one in the Book of Acts, but the Acts of the Holy Ghost including miracles and healings have continued as we have shewn in our ninth chapter: "The Canon of Scripture Closed: the Dispensation of the Holy Ghost continues."

Healing reserved for the Millennium?

Question:

Is it not correct to say that the gift of healing is reserved for the millennial age?

Answer:

In the Millennium, Satan, the author of disease, will be bound, the curse removed, sin, the cause of disease, almost unknown, and life will be so prolonged that those a hundred years of age will be considered children. Consequently there will be little, if any, need of healing. To withhold the gift of healing when the world is full of diseased folk, and to bestow it when there will be few, if any, does not seem like God's usual gracious way of dealing with mankind.

> And he laid hold on the dragon, that old serpent, which is the devil, and Satan, and bound him a thousand years,
> And cast him into the bottomless pit, and shut him up, and set a seal upon him, that he should deceive the nations no more, till the thousand years should be fulfilled . . .
> —Rev. xx. 2, 3.

Perpetuated throughout the present dispensation.

Question:

Have you any further definite scripture proof to shew that the gift of healing was to be perpetuated throughout the Christian dispensation?

Answer:

Yes! Our Lord in the 16th chapter of Mark definitely included healing in His promise to the Church of the future. His ministers were commissioned to preach the Gospel in the whole world and to every creature. They were to believe for, and expect, miraculous signs to confirm the message wherever it was proclaimed.

> And He said unto them, Go ye into all the world, and preach the Gospel to every creature.
>
> He that believeth and is baptised shall be saved; but he that believeth not shall be damned.
>
> And these signs shall follow them that believe: In My Name shall they cast out devils; they shall speak with new tongues;
>
> They shall take up serpents; and if they drink any deadly thing it shall not hurt them; they shall lay hands on the sick, and they shall recover.
>
> So then after the Lord had spoken unto them, He was received up into heaven, and sat on the right hand of God.
>
> And they went forth and preached everywhere, the Lord working with them, and confirming the Word with signs following. Amen.—Mark xvi. 15-20.

Healing for the twelve tribes.

Question:

As the Epistle of James was written to the twelve tribes scattered abroad, is it correct to say that the promise of healing in the 5th chapter was exclusively for them, and not for the Church to-day?

Answer:

Peter's Epistle begins thus: '' Peter, an apostle of Jesus Christ to the strangers scattered throughout Pontus, Galatia, Cappadocia, Asia and Bithynia." John writes to " an elect lady," and Paul to " the saints that be in Rome." By the same line of reasoning one must conclude that these Epistles, if exclusively so addressed, are not applicable to the Christian Church of the twentieth century, and further it suggests that the Church of to-day has no right to appropriate scriptures from any other Epistle at all, for there is not a single epistle addressed to the Church of Christ " in the twentieth century." The Church of Christ consists of all who are born of the Spirit of God in every age.

> Is any sick among you? let him call for the elders of the church; and let them pray over him, anointing him with oil in the Name of the Lord;
> And the prayer of faith shall save the sick, and the Lord shall raise him up; and if he have committed sins, they shall be forgiven him.— James v. 14, 15.

Sickness the result of sin.

Question:

Did sickness and disease come into the world through sin?

Answer:

The Bible definitely shews that death came into the world as a result of Adam's sin, and it is quite reasonable to determine that sickness and disease, the processes which lead to death, also came into the world as a result of sin.

> Wherefore as by one man sin entered into the world, and death by sin; and so death passed upon all men, for that all have sinned.—Rom. v. 12.

Sickness and personal sin.

Question:

Does personal sin sometimes result in disease?

Answer:

Scripture certainly teaches that a person can suffer in body as a direct result of personal sin.

> Fools because of their transgression, and because of their iniquities, are afflicted.—Psalm cvii. 17.

Sickness attributable to natural causes.

Question:

Is there not a tremendous amount of sickness in the world to-day attributable to natural and physical causes that has no direct connection with Adam's sin?

Answer:

Sickness may and does arise from unhealthy conditions in which people live, from bodily weaknesses that are natural in different periods of life, and from harmful conditions under which they are called to labour. But it will be well to remember that life under such circumstances is the indirect result of sin. Who could possibly visualise unhealthy conditions of living and labour, or even the present disturbed state of the elements, in the garden of Eden before the fall of man? If the first cause of these hurtful conditions was sin, it is only reasonable to assume that sickness arising from such conditions is indirectly the result of sin. In the future state when sin will have been destroyed, conditions and circumstances of life will be vastly different from what they are at present, for there will be no sickness, no disease, and no death.

> And God shall wipe away all tears from their eyes; and there shall be no more death, neither sorrow, nor crying, neither shall there be any more pain : for the former things are passed away.—Rev. xxi. 4.

Derangement of physical law without breach of moral law.

Question:

Is it not possible that Adam, in the unfallen creation, could have acted in such a way as would inevitably result in the derangement of physical laws, without actually committing sin?

151

Answer:

Sin in the Garden of Eden was actually the derangement of a physical law. When God made man, He gave the body its natural desires and appetites, which were holy, and the satisfying of which was quite legitimate. The transgression consisted in allowing the natural desire to be enticed and drawn away, until it crossed the boundary line which God had specifically established. The suggestion of sickness and disease being the possible result of some things Adam might have done without breach of the moral law, opens up avenues of conjecture that had better be left unexplored. Even a mediæval penman in such circumstances would say, " Let not thy curiosity lead thee where I cannot guide thee." But we have in the sure Word of prophecy the right attitude to adopt in questions of this kind. " The secret things belong unto the Lord our God : but those things which are revealed belong unto us and to our children for ever, that we may do all the words of this law " (Deut. xxix. 29).

> And the Lord commanded the man, saying, Of every tree of the garden thou mayest freely eat :
> But of the tree of the knowledge of good and evil, thou shalt not eat of it : for in the day that thou eatest thereof thou shalt surely die.—Gen. ii. 16, 17.
> Whosoever committeth sin transgresseth also the law : for sin is the transgression of the law.—I. John iii. 4.

Miracles & Healings in Present Dispensation

Iniquities of fathers in third and fourth generations.

Question:

If the Scripture teaches that the iniquity of the fathers shall be visited upon the children unto the third and fourth generations, what hope is there of healing for those who are suffering under this visitation?

Answer:

You should read the context of the scripture referred to. Taking for granted that physical disorder is implied by the iniquity of the fathers, the context clearly shews that it is visited upon those that hate God, and that He shews mercy unto those that love Him and keep His commandments. All are invited to participate in the blessing of healing, for God keeps His covenant and mercy with them that love Him and keep His commandments, to a thousand generations.

> Thou shalt not bow down thyself to them, nor serve them: for I the Lord thy God am a jealous God, visiting the iniquity of the fathers upon the children unto the third and fourth generation of them that hate Me;
> And shewing mercy unto thousands of them that love Me, and keep My commandments.—Exodus xx. 5, 6.
> Know therefore that the Lord thy

God, He is God, the faithful God, which keepeth covenant and mercy with them that love Him and keep His commandments to a thousand generations.—Deut. vii. 9.

Healing in the Atonement.

Question:

Is healing provided for the body in the Atonement?

Answer:

The atoning and redeeming work of Christ on the cross is the sovereign remedy for all the evil effects of the first Adam's disobedience, which include sickness and disease. Paul in his letter to the Colossians eloquently testifies to this certainty as follows : " In whom we have redemption through His blood, even the forgiveness of sins : . . . And, having made peace through the blood of His Cross, by Him to reconcile all things unto Himself ; by Him, I say, whether they be things in earth, or things in heaven." Bodily healing is one of the present-day benefits of that atoning and redeeming work.

Is any sick among you? let him call for the elders of the church; and let them pray over him, anointing him with oil in the Name of the Lord :

And the prayer of faith shall save the sick, and the Lord shall raise him up; and if he have committed sins, they shall be forgiven him.—James v. 14, 15.

Gradual and instantaneous healing.

Question:

Are we correct in concluding that God heals gradually as well as instantaneously?

Answer:

The gifts of healing are amongst the nine miraculous gifts that are distributed to the Church by the Holy Spirit. The word *healing* suggests a gradual recovery, and many are restored in this way. Another among the nine gifts is the working of miracles, which suggests an immediate Divine interposition, so that a person is instantaneously healed. In our Lord's own ministry there were these two kinds of healings.

> Jesus saith unto him, Go thy way; thy son liveth. And the man believed the word that Jesus had spoken unto him, and he went his way.
>
> And as he was now going down, his servants met him, and told him, saying, Thy son liveth.
>
> Then enquired he of them the hour when he *began to amend.* And they said unto him, Yesterday at the seventh hour the fever left him.
>
> So the father knew that it was at the same hour, in the which Jesus

155

said unto him, Thy son liveth : and himself believed, and his whole house.—John iv. 50-53.

And when He saw them, He said unto them, Go shew yourselves unto the priests. And it came to pass, that, as they went, they were cleansed.—Luke xvii. 14.

And it came to pass, when He was in a certain city, behold a man full of leprosy : who seeing Jesus fell on his face, and besought Him, saying, Lord, if Thou wilt, Thou canst make me clean. And He put forth His hand, and touched him, saying, I will : be thou clean. And *immediately* the leprosy departed from him.—Luke v. 12, 13.

Seekers after salvation : seekers after healing.

Question:

Why do all who truly seek salvation find it, yet all who truly seek bodily healing do not find it?

Answer:

All persons who truly seek salvation are sure of finding it because it is definitely stated in Scripture that it is God's will for all, without exception, to be saved. It is impossible for a person to remain unsaved and be in the will of God.

> For this is good and acceptable in the sight of God our Saviour;

> Who will have all men to be
> saved, and to come unto the know-
> ledge of the truth.—I. Tim. ii. 3, 4.

Although bodily healing is one of the present benefits of the atoning work of Christ on the cross, the Scripture definitely shews that all who truly seek bodily healing do not find it. It is possible for a person to be suffering from some physical infirmity, and yet be in the will of God.

> And He said unto me, My grace
> is sufficient for thee: for My strength
> is made perfect in weakness. Most
> gladly therefore will I rather glory
> in my infirmities, that the power of
> Christ may rest upon me.
> Therefore I take pleasure in infir-
> mities, in reproaches, in necessities,
> in persecutions, in distresses for
> Christ's sake: for when I am weak,
> then am I strong.—II. Cor. xii. 9, 10.

Natural law of healing accelerated.

Question:

Does the scripture condemn a child of God who uses natural curative means when praying for the healing of his body?

Answer:

Some of the most spiritual saints who pray for healing feel quite free to co-operate with the natural law of healing in the use of natural curative means. This attitude is sanctioned in Scripture, for Paul prescribed means for Timothy's " often infirmities." Prayer and co-ordination with the natural law of healing, which is inherent in human nature, often results in its acceleration, and healing has come with astonishing speed. We have frequently come into contact with saints who have testified to marvellous healing results in this way. Others have felt definitely led of God to abandon all natural curative means, and they too have testified to astounding miracles of healing in answer to prayer. We do not presume to dictate to saints in this matter, for it is one that must be decided by themselves. But we do advise all to act wisely concerning the law of cleansing against contagion, and the law of isolation against infection, which were undoubtedly embodied in the "statutes" mentioned in the great Healing Covenant of Exodus xxv.

> Drink no longer water, but use a little wine for thy stomach's sake and thine often infirmities.—I. Tim. v. 23.

Mixture of grace and works.

Question:

If healing is of grace, is there not the danger of mixing works and grace by using natural curative means?

Answer:

Salvation is entirely of grace, but most natural means are legitimately used in order that men may experience it. Buildings are erected, organisations formed, and preachers are trained; yet works are not mixed with grace by so doing.

King Asa and curative means.

Question:

Did King Asa die because he used natural curative means?

Answer:

The sin of King Asa consisted in closing God out of his life when he was sick. He had previously known the mighty power of God, yet he deliberately turned to the physicians of heathendom, and ignored the God of Israel. The words, " sought not to the Lord " clearly shew that he shut God out of his sick chamber, hence the dire result. The sick person in this twentieth century who chooses to follow the example of this king and shuts God out of his life, to depend entirely upon natural curative means need not expect God's help or blessing to recover.

> And Asa in the thirty and ninth year of his reign was diseased in his feet, until his disease was exceeding great : yet in his disease he sought not to the Lord, but to the physicians.—II. Chron. xvi. 12.

Healing Rays

Healings: do they last?

Question:

Is it true that present-day healings do not last?

Answer:

The twelfth chapter of this book furnishes an up-to-date answer to this question. We can expect the healings to last as long as the healed ones walk with God. There appears to be a very close link between spiritual life and bodily health.

> Beloved, I wish above all things that thou mayest prosper and be in health, even as thy soul prospereth. —III. John 2.

Claim victory over death.

Question:

If the power to heal the sick is for the Church to-day, why not claim victory over death and raise the dead?

Answer:

Immunity from death is promised to every believer who is alive at the time of Christ's return. Nothing is impossible with God. He can give victory over death in this present dispensation, but He does not promise to do so until the second advent of Christ.

> The last enemy that shall be destroyed is death.—I. Cor. xv, 26.

Patriarchs, prophets, apostles, who believed in the truth and experience of Divine healing and health have passed away. Some came to the end of life's journey like as a shock of corn cometh in its season. Others whose lives were cut short glorified God by wearing the martyr's crown.

> And Moses was an hundred and twenty years old when he died; his eye was not dim, nor his natural force abated.—Deut. xxxiv. 7.

Death to the believer, at any time, simply means falling asleep, for its fear has been destroyed. There is no intimation in the Bible that he must fall asleep as a result of disease.

> Forasmuch then as the children are partakers of flesh and blood, He also Himself likewise took part of the same; that through death He might destroy him that had the power of death, that is, the devil;
> And deliver them who through fear of death were all their lifetime subject to bondage.—Heb. ii. 14, 15.

God could certainly confirm the preaching of the Word in our day by raising the dead, but this is not included in the definite signs that were promised to confirm the Gospel message, whereas healing for the body is included.

> And these signs shall follow them that believe. In My Name shall they cast out devils; they shall speak with

new tongues. They shall take up serpents, and if they drink any deadly
thing it shall not hurt them; they
shall lay hands on the sick and they
shall recover.—Mark xvi, 17, 18.

Paul's thorn an argument for Divine healing.

Question:

Why teach that all who walk in obedience
to God's will can claim healing for the body,
when Paul, whose life was an example of
obedience, was not healed?

Answer:

One cannot be dogmatic concerning the nature
of Paul's thorn in the flesh. Taking for granted
that the messenger of Satan which buffeted
him was some physical infirmity, Paul under
the circumstances set a fine example of importunate prayer and faith in Divine healing. He
manifested implicit faith in his claim to deliverance by presenting it until the revelation came
that he was to suffer. He actually sought
deliverance three times, and there is every
reason for assuming that he would have kept
on seeking if the Divine will had not been
revealed. Paul's attitude towards his thorn in
the flesh, instead of being an argument against
Divine healing, is a weighty one in its favour.
We maintain that every child of God, provided
he complies with relative conditions, can

162

rightly seek healing, unless he is assured that it is God's will for him to suffer.

> And lest I should be exalted above measure through the abundance of the revelations, there was given to me a thorn in the flesh, the messenger of Satan to buffet me, lest I should be exalted above measure.
>
> For this thing I besought the Lord thrice that it might depart from me.
>
> And He said unto me, My grace is sufficient for thee: for My strength is made perfect in weakness. Most gladly therefore will I rather glory in my infirmities, that the power of Christ may rest upon me.—II. Cor. xii. 7-9.

Signs an evidence that faith is lacking.

Question:

Is not the seeking of signs on the part of a Christian evidence in itself of lacking faith, and is not the highest level of faith that which receives without feeling or experience?

Answer:

The Christian religion is essentially a religion of faith that produces signs, *e.g.,* when a sinner repents and believes (exercises faith) in the Lord Jesus Christ, he becomes a new creature in Christ. The signs of a new life come as a result of his faith. If a sinner professed faith in Christ as Saviour, and manifested the old life as he formerly used to, one would soon doubt his conversion. Surely you are not going to say that the latter lived on a higher level of faith than the former. Peter certainly expected a sign when he commanded the lame man of Acts iii. to rise in the Name of Jesus Christ of Nazareth. In the light of the above argument, Peter lacked in faith somewhere because the sign of healing followed the command. Again, the disciples in the upper room at Jerusalem must have been living on the lower level of faith, because the whole one hundred and twenty had miraculous signs when they were baptised with the Holy Ghost.

> And the word of God increased; and the number of the disciples multiplied in Jerusalem greatly; and a great company of the priests were obedient to the faith.
>
> And Stephen, full of faith and power, did great wonders and miracles among the people.—Acts vi. 7, 8.
>
> Even so, faith, if it hath not works, is dead, being alone.
>
> Yea, a man may say, Thou hast faith, and I have works: shew me thy faith without thy works, and I will shew thee my faith by my works.—James ii. 17, 18.

Not all healed.

Question:

Why are some of the people who seek healing at your revival and healing campaigns not healed?

164

Answer:

There are many reasons such as are mentioned in the next answer. All were not healed in the days of our Lord.

> And He could there do no mighty work, save that He laid His hands upon a few sick folk, and healed them. And He marvelled because of their unbelief . . .—Mark vi. 5, 6.

Failure attributable to lack of faith.

Question:

Do you attribute failure on the part of those who are not healed to lack of faith?

Answer:

We do not attribute all failures to the lack of faith. There might be other reasons why people are not healed. Hindrances in the lives of seekers, and unwillingness to obey the commandments of the Lord, can hinder the work of healing. Again some are allowed to suffer for disciplinary and other purposes. See Paul's thorn on page 162, and also the instruction at the end of this chapter.

Revival and healing campaigns.

Question:

What authority is there in Scripture for holding large revival and healing campaigns?

Healing Rays

Answer:

The Acts of the Apostles is a record of revival and healing campaigns, news of which was noised abroad. A most glorious revival started on the Day of Pentecost—three thousand souls are saved, a lame man is healed, five thousand men believe, signs, wonders, and miracles of healing are in evidence everywhere. Philip entered Samaria, preached Christ, there were converts, healings, miracles, until the whole city was stirred.

And by the hands of the apostles were many signs and wonders wrought among the people . . .

And believers were the more added to the Lord, multitudes both of men and women.

There came also a multitude out of the cities round about unto Jerusalem, bringing sick folks, and them which were vexed with unclean spirits : and they were healed every one.— Acts v. 12, 14, 16.

Then Philip went down to the city of Samaria, and preached Christ unto them.

And the people with one accord gave heed unto those things which Philip spake, hearing and seeing the miracles which he did.

For unclean spirits, crying with loud voice, came out of many that were possessed with them : and many taken with palsies, and that were lame, were healed.

And there was great joy in that city.—Acts viii. 5-8.

166

STEPS LEADING TO HEALING

Be sure you are in line with God's will.

> And this is the confidence that we have in Him, that, if we ask anything according to His will, He heareth us.—1. John v. 14.

If unsaved you should be saved.

> For this is good and acceptable in the sight of God our Saviour; who will have all men to be saved, and to come unto the knowledge of the truth. —I. Tim. ii. 3, 4.

If you are a backslider, get restored.

> O Israel, return unto the Lord thy God; for thou hast fallen by thine iniquity.
>
> I will heal their backsliding, I will love them freely: for Mine anger is turned away from him.—Hosea xiv. 1, 4.
>
> If My people, which are called by My Name, shall humble themselves, and pray, and seek My face, and turn from their wicked ways; then will I hear from heaven, and will forgive their sin, and will heal their land.— II. Chron. vii. 14.

Be sure to obey the commandments of God.

> If ye love Me, keep My commandments.—John xiv. 15.

If you are saved you should be baptised.

> And he commanded them to be bap-
> tised in the Name of the Lord . , .
> —Acts x. 48.

If you are saved you should remember the Lord's death.

> And when He had given thanks,
> He brake it, and said, Take, eat:
> this is My body, which is broken for
> you: this do in remembrance of Me.
>
> After the same manner also He took
> the cup, when He had supped, say-
> ing, This cup is the new testament
> in My blood: this do ye, as oft as
> ye drink it, in remembrance of Me.
>
> For as often as ye eat this bread,
> and drink this cup, ye do shew the
> Lord's death till He come.—I. Cor.
> xi. 24-26.

If you are saved you should bring your tithes into the storehouse.

> Bring ye all the tithes into the
> storehouse, that there may be meat
> in Mine house, and prove Me now
> herewith, saith the Lord of hosts,
> if I will not open you the windows
> of heaven, and pour you out a bless-
> ing, that there shall not be room
> enough to receive it.
>
> And I will rebuke the devourer
> for your sakes, and he shall not des-
> troy the fruits of your ground;
> neither shall your vine cast her fruit
> before the time in the field, saith the
> Lord of hosts.—Mal. iii. 10, 11.

Be sure you confess any wrongdoing to those you have injured.

> Confess your faults one to another, and pray one for another, that ye may be healed.—James v. 16.

You should manifest love to other Christians.

> Seeing ye have purified your souls in obeying the truth through the Spirit unto unfeigned love of the brethren, see that ye love one another with a pure heart fervently.—I. Peter i. 22.

HINDRANCES IN THE WAY OF HEALING

Unbelief:

> But Jesus said unto them, A prophet is not without honour, but in his own country, and among his own kin, and in his own house.
>
> And He could there do no mighty work, save that He laid His hands upon a few sick folk, and healed them.
>
> And He marvelled because of their unbelief . . .—Mark vi. 4-6.

Seeking healing for self-gratification.

> Ye ask, and receive not, because ye ask amiss, that ye may consume it upon your lusts.—James iv. 3.

Being guilty of personal sins:

> If I regard iniquity in my heart, the Lord will not hear me.—Psalm lxvi. 18.

MODES OF HEALING

The direct appeal on the part of an individual:

> And, behold, there came a leper and worshipped Him, saying, Lord, if Thou wilt, Thou canst make me clean.—Matt. viii. 2.

The co-operation and fellowship of practical sympathisers :

> And when they could not come nigh unto Him for the press, thy uncovered the roof where He was: and when they had broken it up, they let down the bed wherein the sick of the palsy lay.
>
> When Jesus saw their faith . . . —Mark ii. 4, 5.

The co-operation and mutual fellowship of prayer warriors :

> Again I say unto you, That if two of you shall agree on earth as touchany thing that they shall ask, it shall be done for them of My Father which is in heaven.—Matt. xviii. 19.

The laying on of hands :

> . . . They shall lay hands on the sick, and they shall recover.—Mark xvi. 18.

The anointing with oil :

> Is any sick among you? let him call for the elders of the church; and let them pray over him, anointing him with oil in the Name of the Lord.—James v. 14.

The going forth of God's Word :

> He sent His word, and healed them, and delivered them from their destructions.—Psalm cvii. 20.

The ministry of prayer in the Church :

> By stretching forth Thine hand to heal; and that signs and wonders may be done by the Name of Thy holy Child Jesus.—Acts iv. 30.

THINGS TO REMEMBER WHEN SEEKING HEALING

That the state of your spiritual life can easily affect the condition of your body; therefore see that your spiritual life is nourished by prayer, and the reading of God's Word.

> Is any among you afflicted? let him pray . . .—James v. 13.
> This is my comfort in my affliction: for Thy word hath quickened me.—Psalm cxix. 50.

That healing, like salvation, is all of grace, therefore do not consider your own worthiness.

> He that spared not His own Son, but delivered Him up for us all, how shall He not with Him also freely give us all things?—Rom, viii. 32.

That you should not worry over your little faith, but consider the greatness of the Divine Physician.

> And the Lord said, If ye had faith as a grain of mustard seed, ye might say unto this sycamine tree, Be thou plucked up by the root, and be thou planted in the sea; and it should obey you.—Luke xvii. 6.

That you must not be overburdened about your long-standing disease. Cases like yours have been healed before.

> And, behold, there was a woman which had a spirit of infirmity eighteen years, and was bowed together, and could in no wise lift up herself.
> And He laid His hands on her: and immediately she was made straight, and glorified God.—Luke xiii. 11, 13.

That you must not be discouraged if not immediately healed. Yours might be a gradual recovery.

> Then enquired he of them the hour when he began to amend. And they said unto him, Yesterday at the seventh hour the fever left him.— John iv. 52.

That due attention must be given to the laws of health as to food, hygiene, bodily exercise, and rest.

> If thou wilt . . . give ear to His commandments, and keep all His statutes , . . . I am the Lord that healeth thee.—Exodus xv. 26.

That a cheerful heart is a tonic to yourself and to others, therefore cultivate a happy disposition.

> A merry heart doeth good like a medicine.—Prov. xvii. 22.

That God is glorified and His works made manifest when the supernatural is in evidence.

> Jesus answered, Neither hath this man sinned, nor his parents : but that the works of God should be made manifest in him.
>
> I must work the works of Him that sent Me, while it is day : the night cometh, when no man can work.—John ix. 3, 4.
>
> This beginning of miracles did Jesus in Cana of Galilee, *and manifested forth His glory;* and His disciples believed on Him.—John ii. 11,

173

CHAPTER XII

Healings and Miracles in Our Day

For we cannot but speak the things which we have seen and heard.—Acts iv. 20.

PRESENT-DAY testimonies of healing can easily be undervalued, for they do not suggest the mystery and wonderment that are associated with miracles in days gone by. The healing of a cripple in the days of the apostles always seems a greater wonder than the healing of one who also stands perfectly whole in our midst. The men, too, of the past who were used as channels of blessing to the sick and suffering, seemed to be covered with haloes that are altogether missing in the ordinary channels of to-day. These thoughts were probably in the heart of the inspired writer when, meditating upon the chronicles of faith in the life of Elijah, he declared that mighty prophet to be a man " subject to like passions as we are. " There is a tendency to underestimate the glorious operations of the Spirit, and we are continually comparing the revivals of to-day with those that are recorded in history. Human nature has not changed since the days of our Lord, for it is ever ready to build sepulchres to the prophets of the past, while even persecuting those of the present. During these latter years God has graciously poured out His Spirit in prayer-laden and power-permeated gatherings throughout the land. Tens of thousands have been converted, thousands baptised, and lives and homes everywhere have been transformed. Multitudes have been healed, and miracles just as marvellous as those recorded in the Acts of the Apostles have been witnessed before wondering crowds. In these gatherings both rich and poor, the learned and the unlearned, the high and the humble have come under the healing rays of the Sun of Righteousness. The testimonies of healing miracles which are given in this chapter are only a few of the many who have stood the test of years. Some of them, as we shall see, were helpless and hopeless cripples until they were miraculously healed after hands had been laid upon them according to the 16th chapter of Mark, and they were anointed with oil according to the 5th chapter of James. Some of these miracles of healing were witnessed by thousands of people, and their testimonies given before monster congregations in the largest halls throughout the British Isles, including the Royal Albert Hall, Crystal Palace and Alexandra Palace, London, and the Bingley Exhibition Building in Birmingham. We are allowing some of the healed ones to tell their own story of suffering and healing, each one in his or her own way.

175

HEALED OF INSANITY.

The story of Mrs. Smith of Seven Kings should encourage faith in God for the deliverance of mental cases. We have often advised people to send for the nearest godly servant of Christ, as well as for the physician, when a loved one shews signs of insanity.

" I gladly give my testimony with thankfulness of heart to God for what He has done for me. About three years ago a great trouble came into my life which broke me down completely. I became a physical and mental wreck. All my friends despaired of my life. I could not sleep for weeks and could eat scarcely any food. I was taken to three different doctors who prescribed medicine, etc., for me, but I gradually got worse until I became hopelessly insane. But my mother never ceased praying for me, and although she went through great suffering she never lost faith in God. Time went on and mother was advised to get me away to a home or an asylum as I could not be trusted alone—and had to be tied down to my bed at night, until one day my sister came home and told mother she had heard there was a faith-healer at Barking who healed people through prayer, but mother could not get me to go to the meetings—I was in such an awful state—and her heart was nearly broken. Then she heard that Principal George Jeffreys was conducting a Revival and

Healing Campaign at the East Ham Town Hall. With great difficulty mother got me there and on to the platform. I was prayed for : the power of God fell upon me and I was completely delivered. I was restored to perfect health, my reason was restored, and I have been well ever since. I am a living testimony to the healing power of the Lord Jesus Christ.''

MRS. A. E. SMITH'S MOTHER'S TESTIMONY.

I am very pleased to be able to confirm my daughter's testimony of how God marvellously healed her of insanity. There is no need for me to repeat any details, but I wish it to be known that before my daughter's trouble she was living away from me but in the same district. When her trouble came upon her, she came to live with me, and I personally had to see to her. God alone knows what I went through. My experience was absolutely terrible, never knowing from one moment to another what was going to happen. Words cannot express my feelings. How the Lord stood by me and gave me strength to hang on to Him in prayer. There is one thing my daughter omitted in her testimony, and that is the number of times she had attempted her life ; but God brought someone on the scene just at the right time to prevent her. I can confirm all that my daughter has said. To God be all the glory ! ''—*Mrs. H. Harper* (Chadwell).

177

Healing Rays

HELPLESS CRIPPLE WALKS OUT OF WHEELED CARRIAGE AT SOUTHAMPTON.

Miss Florence Munday of Southampton was raised from her wheeled carriage at one of our services in the Wesleyan Central Hall, Southampton, in May, 1927, after suffering for fourteen years. Her life has since been devoted to the service of Christ, and her stirring testimony has been the means of bringing souls into the Kingdom, and of leading suffering ones into the truth of Divine healing.

" Fourteen years ago I fell, and tubercular trouble set up in my knee. During these years I had never been able to stand or walk. Together with this I suffered from a dreadful skin disease, which started when I was a tiny child, twenty-nine years ago. At times I had both arms from wrists to shoulders covered with bandages. I used to faint when the dressings had to come off and the hot foments put on. The knee became worse as time went on, and I suffered agony from the various splints and bandages I had to wear. I have sometimes been lying in bed without springs, while my leg was in the iron splint and my foot encased. After that experience, the iron splint was discarded for a plaster one. Two doctors spent two hours moulding this splint. It was composed of sixty yards of bandage and over fourteen pounds of plaster of Paris. It took one week to dry, only to crack at the end, when more bandages had to be applied, and more plaster moulded on. I was in terrible pain, my leg got worse, and with the continual changes of the splints to fit my wasting leg, I suffered agony. The doctor gave no hope and advised amputation ; worse still, it would have to be taken off so high up that no stump was to be left, so that I could not wear an artificial limb.

" On Wednesday, 4th May, 1927, my sisters came home after attending one of Principal George Jeffreys' revival meetings at the Wesleyan Central Hall, Southampton. They brought the news that a lady had stepped out of her bath chair that very day in the service. They asked me to go, and I nervously agreed to do so. I was pushed there in my bath chair, and wheeled right up to the front of the service. It was a service I shall never forget. The missioner came to me and asked me if I believed God could heal me. I said, " Yes ! but I am in a splint." His answer was, " God can certainly heal you, even if you are in a splint." I was anointed with oil, and as he prayed, my whole body vibrated with life. I was under the power of God. My leg moved up and down three times in the splint, and soon I was able to sit up. All pain was gone. I was healed. I stood up and stepped out of my bath chair without aid. I was on my feet for the first time after fourteen years. I walked around that big building three times. My leg was like that of a frail baby's when the splint was taken off ; and altogether the leg was 4½ inches shorter than the other. Now they are both the same size, quite normal. You can understand how I feel, when I tell you I want to sing all day : ' Jesus, Thou art everything to me.' "

HELPLESS CRIPPLE HEALED.

Mr. James Gregson was miraculously healed at Leeds in April, 1927. The day of his sudden recovery will long be remembered by the great crowds who witnessed the miracle. An absolute cripple, whose only power of loco-motion was painfully to propel himself along the ground dragging his twisted legs behind him.

" I was an iron-maker by trade. On 2nd February, 1922, I met with a serious accident. I fell from a height into a coal-box, every bone being shifted out of place. My spine was also injured. I was taken to the hospital, where I received every treatment that the hospital could supply, but I became a helpless, hopeless cripple. I had to creep along the ground ; my legs were twisted and I dragged them along in a crossed position. I could not sit, but had to lie. My life was a misery.

"My wife on the Wednesday evening read in

the paper an account of a woman who was blind receiving her sight in Principal George Jeffreys' campaign meetings. As she read, I was convinced that I could be healed if only I could go to the meeting. I went on the Saturday on my crutches, dragging my legs behind. That night I was saved : He forgave all my iniquities. I then went again on the Sunday to the Coliseum. God alone knows how I got there, and when I got there I had a great struggle to get in, but some of the people took pity on me and dragged me round to the back. Then the attendants carried me in and laid me in front of the platform.

One of the revival party came to me and said : " Brother, you don't look comfortable ; can I make you more comfortable ? " and I answered, " I am never comfortable," for I was in pain night and day. I was prayed for by the Principal, and when he laid his hands upon me I felt as if a dozen hands were placed all over my body and I felt every bone going back into place. I was instantly released and I was completely healed. I was only skin and bone, my eyes were sunk in my head. Inside two weeks I had gained two stone five pounds, and I continued to put on flesh. I was able to go back to my work as strong as ever. I have never lost a day's work since through ill-health. Hallelujah ! To God be all the glory ! Praise the Lord ! "

SLEEPING SICKNESS, BLINDNESS AND SEIZURE HEALED AT PORTSMOUTH.

Miss C. Jardine, of Portsmouth, is another case of miraculous healing that occurred during the Portsmouth campaign, 1927. She was wheeled to our services in a carriage, her body was twisted up as a result of sleeping sickness, so that her chin was touching her knee, and she was completely blind in one eye. The Lord healed her, and her story of healing and deliverance has led others to Christ for salvation and healing.

" For twenty years I suffered from internal paralysis caused through a fright. During these years I suffered terrible agonies of pain, and had three serious operations. After the second one the surgeon told me I could never work again. I lay at death's door in hospital for weeks, but I never lost faith in the Lord Jesus Christ. I also had a tubercular knee and nearly lost my leg, but I praise and thank God He spoke to my mother, and she would not consent to the operation ; but the surgeon removed a piece of diseased bone, and left me with a stiff joint. I suffered torture in trying to get that joint to bend, and no doctor could do it. I was in hospital several times, and everything was done for me that could be done. Once when I came round from the anæsthetic my knee was quite black with bruises, and I endured terrible agony for weeks, not being able to bear even a sheet to touch it. I was then put into an iron splint, and an extension to pull the leg down ; but it gradually got worse, and I was put into an iron splint and cork boot, which I had to wear night and day. When this one was taken off I was put into a plaster splint, and eventually into an asbestos one ; but I praise God I do not want any splints now, for my leg that was shorter and wasted is the same as the other one. All these years I was not able to get any rest night or day. I was constantly in pain, but the Lord gave me strength to bear all my pain, and I was happy in the love of Jesus. My trouble did not end here, for three years ago I took sleepy sickness (*encephalitis lethargia*). I was unconscious for three weeks, and I went totally blind. The sight came back into my right eye, but the left one was eaten away, and the doctors said I could never see again with that eye. I had one of the best and most attentive doctors that anyone could possibly have. He attended me night and day. May God bless him, and all who did so much for me. Then I had a seizure which twisted me up, and I shall never forget the agony I went through when the doctor came and stretched all the muscles of my body. When I got to my feet I discovered I could not straighten myself, and my left leg was twisted right around, while my head almost touched my knees. On 22nd September, 1927, I was wheeled in my bath chair to

Principal George Jeffreys' healing meeting, was prayed for and anointed by him in the Name of the Lord, and was healed. I felt the power of God go through my body. My spine is quite straight now, and the sight has come back to my blind eye. Glory to God! Hallelujah!

" I now go to bed to sleep, not to lie in pain all night. Praise His holy Name! I am able to eat almost anything now, after seven or eight years on patent foods. I cannot praise God enough for all the blessings He has bestowed upon me, and I am happy in His service. I hope that this testimony may be a blessing and a help to some poor sufferer. To God be all the glory! "

CURED OF EPILEPTIC FITS AFTER THIRTY-FOUR YEARS OF SUFFERING.

Mrs. Appleton, who suffered for thirty-four years from epileptic fits, was healed at Leeds in May, 1927. Her testimony should encourage those who are suffering from epilepsy. In the latter part of 1931 we heard her testify that she had been free from fits ever since.

" I am sending you my testimony along, as I think it is only right after suffering for thirty-four years with epileptic fits and kidney trouble. I have been under many doctors and also had treatment at the Leeds dispensary, but I got no better. When I heard that Principal George Jeffreys was holding revival and healing services at the Salem Central Hall, Leeds, I decided to go. I was anointed and prayed for, and as soon as he laid his hands upon me I felt the power of God. This power remained on me for about twenty minutes. I was perfectly healed and I do praise God I have not had a fit since. For ever I shall serve Him. Glory to His Name!

A MODERN MIRACLE. CANCER ROOTED OUT BY THE POWER OF GOD.

Mrs. Paul, of Croydon, had a remarkable experience during our campaign held in that town in April, 1928. She was suffering from cancer, the power of God came upon her and she felt the cancer being removed.

" For fourteen years I have been a great sufferer with gastric ulcers and chronic indigestion which ended in cancer. I was in continual pain night and day. My suffering was so intense that I have often been tempted to end my life. During those years I was continually taking drugs. I spent pounds upon them ; everything was done for me that could be done, but my case was hopeless. I heard of the Revival and Healing Campaign conducted by Principal George Jeffreys in the North End Hall, Croydon. I went to the healing meeting in the afternoon and was prayed for by the Principal. I immediately felt the healing touch, the power of God came upon me and I felt the

185

cords of the cancer being dragged from me and the large lump that I had completely disappeared—not a trace remained. My little girl was prayed for and healed of rheumatism and heart trouble. I don't know how to praise the Lord for all His goodness to myself and my little girl.''

AN INSTANTANEOUS HEALING AT BRIXTON.

TESTIMONY OF THE DEPUTY PRINCIPAL OF BANBURY'S COLLEGE, LEICESTER.

The instantaneous healing of Mr. E. H. Thorpe, Leicester, occurred at the tent campaign held in Brixton, June, 1929. Instead of having a stiff leg for the rest of his life he is completely healed.

'' Seventeen years ago I met with an accident at Grimsby on a ship and fractured my kneecap. The fracture was so complete that all the oil in my knee-cap formed a substance at the bottom of the leg. The infirmary authorities wanted me to have my leg "wired," but I refused and was told I should have a stiff leg for life. I engaged a bone-setter, and although he did his work well, I had temporary paralysis for three months.

'' I attended the healing service at the Brixton Tent held by Principal George Jeffreys on Sunday, 16th June, and I had previously prayed that God would help me to be cured.

" I had been unable for many years to engage in any form of recreation, or walk any distance, and could get up and downstairs only with difficulty and by the aid of the banisters. Within three minutes of the laying-on of hands and the offering of prayer by the Principal, I felt the healing touch of the Divine Master and immediately exclaimed, 'I am healed!' I then rose, again tested the leg, found that I could move it in all directions, that I was able to swing it to and fro, that the ligaments were free (or loose) and that I could kneel without pain on the right knee-cap. I again tested it on the 'bus, running upstairs, and I then had no doubt that the cure was permanent. On arrival in Leicester, I practised running upstairs to the amazement of several who came to visit me.

" At the healing meeting many others gave testimony to being cured of blindness, cancer, consumption and other diseases."

DILATED STOMACH HEALED AT BRIGHTON.

Mr. G. Lelliot, of Worthing, suffered for years with a dilated stomach and was healed at our Campaign in the Dome, Brighton, in June, 1927.

" I have been a sufferer for the past 30 years with a dilated stomach. For 15 years I had to use a stomach pump. I have been to Brighton and Worthing Hospitals, where I had one of the most serious operations. I was prayed for in the Dome at Brighton and completely healed. The next day I had a feeling that something was peeling off my chest, and since then I have had nothing of the old complaint, for which I thank God with all my heart.''

BAPTIST MINISTER'S WIFE HEALED OF CANCER AT BRIGHTON.

Mrs. Algernon Coffin, the wife of a Baptist minister was healed of cancer, dropsy and heart disease at the Royal Pavilion campaign at Brighton in May, 1927.

'' For twenty years I had been a great sufferer. In June, 1917, I saw a specialist, who diagnosed my trouble as cancer ; and on June 9th, 1917, I entered a nursing home for an operation. Twelve months later, the same specialist saw me again, and declared there was a recurrence of the trouble, and that I could not live longer than five months. But in answer to the earnest prayers of many, my life was spared. For many years I had been taking the strongest drugs to alleviate my pain and enable me to sleep. I had not been able to lie down for ten years ; the doctors saw me again and again, and told my dear husband there was no hope whatever. I was in utter despair, the doctors had done all they possibly could for me, but to no avail, and I was given up to die. But, praise God, man's extremity is God's opportunity. By this time dropsy had set in, also heart trouble, and my nerves were in such a state that I could not bear the least sound. Just at this time God sent His dear servant, Principal George Jeffreys, to Brighton, and after much prayer I decided to go to the Divine Healing meeting on the afternoon of May 19th, 1927, in the Royal Pavilion. I was prayed for ; I felt an inward thrill go right through my body, and was instantly met in healing, the evidence being that all my pain ceased, and I was able to sleep ; I also regained my normal size, and never felt anything from the sudden leaving off of the drugs. Two doctors called to see me during the week, and were witnesses to the marvellous change in me. One doctor was amazed when I answered the door to him myself. Coming in, he said, ' What has happened, Mrs. Coffin? Is it really you?' ' Yes, doctor,' I replied, ' I am healed and quite well, after you told me there was no hope. In my helplessness and distress I appealed to a higher One, whose power is not limited. I did not appeal in vain.' The doctor answered, ' Well, it says, " If you ask in faith you shall receive" ; and you certainly have : it is very marvellous. I cannot understand it, but I rejoice with you.' Praise the Name of the Lord, I felt like singing as never before. I have walked miles and travelled about to convey this glad news to others. I have had occasion to praise the Lord, for that terrible disease has never returned. The

Lord has been and ever will be my Great Physician; praise His wonderful Name. I touched by faith the hem of His garment and was made perfectly whole. His power avails to-day."

The following item, taken from the local paper which reported the special meetings held at Glossop in October, 1931, will shew how this sister's remarkable testimony is being confirmed.

" Rev. Algernon Coffin, whose wife had been cured of cancer at one of the Principal's meetings at Brighton, some four years ago, was present at the services this week. A startling incident occurred at the Tuesday afternoon service. The Principal was making reference to the clergyman's wife who had been healed, when a young gentleman stood up at the back of the hall and confirmed the testimony of this remarkable cure. It was ascertained that the young man had, previous to his coming to Glossop, lived only a few doors away from the Rev. Mr. Coffin at Brighton, and had occasionally wheeled Mrs. Coffin about in her invalid chair. The coincident testimony had an electric effect on the congregation. It was found after enquiry, that this gentleman is now the manager of a well-known firm in Glossop."

DELIVERED FROM JACKET, STEEL SUPPORTS, AND BATH CHAIR.

Miss Daisy Noakes, of Seven Kings, wore a jacket and steel supports for head and chin, when suffering from curvature of the spine. After leaving hospital she was wheeled about in a bath chair for three years, was brought to our campaign at Barking in 1925, and **was** miraculously healed.

" I praise God for healing me of curvature of the spine which was caused through a fall when thirteen years old. I was taken to hospital, and had to wear a jacket nearly all of steel. I had steel supports up the back of my head and also under my chin. I wore these for several years, but had to be sent away to hospital, where I remained for a year. I was sent home unable to walk ; and the doctors had another jacket made for me which was all plaster, and reached from my throat to my hips. I was told by the doctor that I should never walk again, and had to be wheeled about in a bath chair for three years. In this condition I was wheeled to Principal George Jeffreys' campaign at Barking and was healed. Thank God, to-day I can walk as well as anyone, have ceased to wear my plaster jacket, and am enjoying the best of health. God gave me a vision a few weeks before I was healed, in which I saw Principal Jeffreys. Imagine my joy when I arrived at the service and saw the same preacher I had seen in my vision. Praise the Lord !''

COMPLETELY HEALED OF ST. VITUS' DANCE AT CLAPHAM.

It is nearly ten years since Mrs. Prentice's little girl, Laura Rose Prentice, was healed at Clapham of St. Vitus' Dance. She was brought to our services by her dear mother and was completely delivered.

" My little girl, Laura Rose Prentice, five years ago suffered with St. Vitus' Dance. The doctor told me she was to be taken away from school, was to be kept from playing with other children, and I was not to allow her to read : she was so ill.

" I took her to Principal George Jeffreys' meetings at Elim Tabernacle, Park Crescent, Clapham. She was anointed and prayed for and was wonderfully healed. I do thank and praise God for His goodness, and I believe there is healing for the body as well as the soul through the finished work of the Lord Jesus on Calvary."

AGONISING SKIN DISEASE HEALED AT HASTINGS AFTER TWELVE YEARS' AGONY.

Mr. H. Ellmer, of Hastings, was a Salvation Army bandsman when he was healed of a terrible skin disease which he had contracted some twelve years before. Like other cases his testimony has been greatly used of God.

" Walking up Queen's Road, Hastings, I saw a bill announcing the healing meetings at the big tent. Being a Salvation Army bandsman, I went out of curiosity, but it did not appeal to me much. I found, however, I was lacking in spiritual things, and I received new light and life at the service.

" I had suffered from an incurable skin disease for twelve years. I suffered agony day and night. I went to one doctor after another, but nothing could be done for me. I went to a healing service, when Principal George Jeffreys prayed for me. I was instantly cured. This was in August, 1927, and I have had no trace of the disease since ; my body is quite clean.

" I have certificates from doctors twelve years ago proving I had the disease, and also a certificate from a doctor to say I haven't got it now. Praise the Lord !"

HELPLESS CRIPPLE HEALED AT LEEDS.

Mrs. Fry, of Leeds, is another bath-chair case. She was quite helpless, and had to be wheeled about in her chair. At our Leeds campaign the sight of her devoted father pushing her chair along to the services had become quite familiar. Needless to say the day she was healed brought great joy to the hearts of both father and daughter.

" I have been in constant pain for years. Half the time of my illness I was quite helpless, and had to be wheeled about in a bath-chair. I came to the healing meeting conducted by Principal George Jeffreys at Leeds, and was wonderfully healed. My body was charged as with electricity, which passed right through my left side, bringing life to my dead nerves. Instead of being wheeled about in a bath-chair I can now do my housework."

ANOTHER BATH-CHAIR CASE AT WIMBLEDON.

Mrs. Gosling, of Tooting, who as an invalid was confined to her home for five years, then wheeled about in a bath chair for another two years before she was brought to our Wimbledon campaign in 1927. Her heart and lips give forth praise to God for her miraculous healing.

" At the age of 37 I had to undergo two operations for moving kidney. I was told I also had enlarged liver and heart trouble. About eight years ago I developed dropsy. I was told by the doctor to make up my mind to be an invalid the rest of my life, as no one on earth could do anything more for me. From that time I was unable to leave the house and was never without medicine. I have been nigh unto death's door about thirty times. On one occasion we had two doctors and they had to prop me up in bed, for if I had laid down I would have died.

"I was brought to Principal George Jeffreys' Revival and Healing Campaign at the Wimbledon Theatre, was prayed for by him, and was completely healed. I went back to the evening service. The great theatre was packed and the only place to obtain a seat was the top gallery. Up I went and found no difficulty in climbing the stairs. Wonder of wonders! After years of suffering—wheeled about in a bath-chair for two years, five years unable to leave the house, the greater time being confined to bed—here I was healed and as a proof was sitting in the top gallery of the Wimbledon Theatre. This was on the 13th of November, 1927, and I have been healed ever since. Praise the Lord!"

GROWTH DISAPPEARS.

Mrs. Trollope, of East Ham, gives her testimony of gradual healing after being ministered to at the Town Hall. Her testimony should encourage those who are not instantly healed.

" I do praise God for healing me of a growth in my throat after I had been under four doctors and then a specialist. The specialist said the growth could not be removed except by an operation.

" I went to the East Ham Town Hall, where Principal George Jeffreys was conducting a revival and healing campaign, and when he prayed for me the growth gradually got less and less and then vanished right away. Praise the Lord!

195   o

" I have the joy of the Lord in my heart, and a peace which passes all understanding. Hallelujah ! "

RUPTURE HEALED AT GLASGOW.

Mrs. Logan, of Glasgow, was healed at our campaign in that city in 1927—being one of many who were healed at that time. Her testimony should encourage the prayer of importunity, for she was healed suddenly after being persistently ministered to.

" It is with grateful heart I give my testimony to a marvellous healing. For eleven years I was an awful sufferer with rupture. During those years I was never without pain. In December, 1926, I became so ill that the doctor was called in. After an examination he said there would have to be an operation. While waiting to go through the operation, I heard that Principal George Jeffreys was conducting a revival and healing campaign in Glasgow. I went to the meeting, and with hundreds of others was anointed and prayed for. I was anointed and prayed for four times. The last time was on Saturday, 10th February, 1927. In the early hours of the following morning, when in bed, the power of God fell upon me, and I was miraculously healed. I called out to my family, ' I am healed.' Oh, what praising of the Lord and rejoicing was in my heart that morning. I waited one week, and then went to the doctor's. I said, ' Doctor, I do not require an operation now.' He asked me why. I told him I had been to the meetings, and I had been prayed for and anointed with oil in the Name of the Lord, and the Lord healed me. ' We shall soon see if you do not,' he said. He then gave me a careful examination, and when finished, he said, ' No, you require no operation,' and added, ' I am going to tell you something I have not told you before. Your operation would not have saved you ; I had little hope of your recovery.' Praise the Lord, I am healed, and have enjoyed the best of health these last few years. To God be all the glory.''

A THANKFUL MOTHER'S TESTIMONY.

THE HEALING OF JOSEPH MACKIE AT GLASGOW.

This thankful mother's testimony should encourage the faith of parents on behalf of their children. Joseph, the son of Mrs. Mackie of Glasgow, was brought by her to the St. Mungo Hall campaign, and was healed on the way home from one of the services.

'' I would like to testify to the goodness of the Lord in healing my son Joseph, at the age of ten.

''For eight and a half years he suffered from septic poisoning which affected his left side, causing him to be quite crippled, until he walked on the side of his foot.

" In February, 1927, a specialist said after a careful examination that he would have to go through an operation, or in a year or two he would be a cripple.

" At this time I heard of the Revival and Healing Campaign going on in the St. Mungo Hall, Glasgow, and decided to go to the meetings. When the invitation was given for those to come forward for healing, Joseph went out of his own accord and was anointed by Principal George Jeffreys and was prayed for.

" We saw no difference until we were almost home, when he suddenly exclaimed, ' Mother ! mother ! I can walk all right now ! ' From that moment there has been no trace of the trouble.

" To God be all the glory ! All things are possible to him that believeth."

MIRACULOUS HEALING OF A HELPLESS CRIPPLE : SPINAL CARRIAGE HAD TO GO.

Miss Edith Scarth, of Leeds, was a victim of tuberculosis of the spine, and had to be laid flat upon her back and wheeled about in a spinal carriage. For 5 years she wore a spinal jacket, and for $3\frac{1}{2}$ years of that period she was obliged to wear a spinal splint which came up to the back of the head, and fastened around the forehead with a strap, to keep the head firmly fixed in one position.

In this condition she was brought to our meetings at Leeds. She heard the soul-thrilling Foursquare Gospel message ; she believed, was prayed for, and was marvellously delivered from the chains of sickness which had long bound her, being gloriously healed.

We give the following story of her suffering and healing in full, so that faith may raise in the hearts of those who are enduring much suffering.

" It is with a heart full of praise and gratitude to God that I write this my testimony to His saving and healing power. I was born in Leeds, and have lived there all my life. When I was only six months old I had consumption of the bowels and was dangerously ill, after which I was very delicate, and in spite of every care on the part of my parents and doctors, was always ailing. I never remember all my life, prior to my healing, being without doctors' medicine, and was often away from school for months together. It was just the same when I started working. I never worked one full year without being away ill. Sometimes I would be away from work for months. When I was nineteen I had a slight hemorrhage, and on examining my lungs the doctors found that I was suffering from consumption. From that time onwards for fifteen years I was a patient at the Leeds Tuberculosis Dispensary, being an inmate of Gateforth Sanatorium three times, Armley Hospital for Consumptives twice, and Killingbeck Hospital three times, for periods varying from three to nine months. For the first six years the trouble was only in my lungs, but I often suffered from pain in my back, and became so round-shouldered that I was compelled to wear shoulder-straps to try and hold my back up. Then a lump formed at the top of my spine, and I was found to be suffering from tuberculosis of the spine. Eighteen months I lay flat on my back, without even a pillow for my head, and had to be wheeled in a spinal carriage. I had to have a spinal jacket which came up to my neck and down to my hips. There was a strap on top of my head to keep my head still, but by pressing on top of my head it made me worse, and had to be taken off. Then sandbags were put at each side of my head to keep it still. After lying down eighteen months I was allowed to get up, and was without my spinal jacket for about a month, but my back became so much worse that it had to be put on again. As time went on, and I grew worse instead of better, new treatments were tried. For nine weeks I lay on my bed, propped up by sandbags, but this made me so much worse that a new kind of splint had to be made. By this time my head was out of place, pushed forward by the disease, and every time I moved my head the bones could be heard clicking. The new splint came right up the back of my head, and fastened round my forehead with a strap, keeping my head firmly fixed in one position, just as if I were in a vice. This, the doctor said, was the only hope of keeping the disease from going to the brain. I wore this splint for $3\frac{1}{2}$ years, only twice being without it, and then for less than twenty-four hours while it was being repaired. Even being without it for so short a time caused such intense pain that the doctor had to give me morphia to numb the pain. Besides wearing these splints, and spending most of my time in bed, I had twice to have fluid taken out of my spine. Once the fluid was pressing on a nerve, and my arm swelled up and was so painful that I had to have it in a splint for a month.

" Then, when my spine had been bad for nine years, I read in the papers of a Revival and Divine Healing Campaign being held in Salem Tabernacle, Leeds, by Principal George Jeffreys, leader of the Foursquare Gospel movement, and of people who were being healed. I was not a bit interested; I simply didn't believe it. But one morning I woke up with an intense desire to go, see, and hear for myself. My mother took me. As the message of salvation was going forth I turned a deaf ear to it. I had always been what is known as a good girl, I had been a Sunday school teacher when I was well enough, but I had to give up my class on account of my health. I had never heard personal salvation preached, and had never seen my need of a personal Saviour. I had always gone to chapel, but I realised my need of something more— I knew not what. Once while in hospital the teaching of confirmation came to my notice, as a result of the visits of a clergyman who regularly gave communion to confirmed folk, and with a view to finding satisfaction I received confirmation, but again there was no satisfaction, there being no change of heart, although I tried to live up to what I had professed.

" I listened to Principal Jeffreys preach, and to his appeal for the salvation of souls. I didn't think I needed salvation, but that all I needed was healing. As I was waiting to be anointed I saw a boy healed who had been paralysed. I saw him lift both his arms up and this encouraged me. I was then anointed, got home, and took off my splint and was without it all night. But next morning my back was so bad I put it on again. I thought there was nothing in it, and did not intend going to the meetings again. This was on the Friday.

" On the Monday I got up again with a longing to go to the meeting. My mother said she would take me. I could hardly wait until it was time. When we got to Salem Tabernacle it was full, we only just managed to get in. This time as the glorious message of salvation was going forth it dawned upon me that after all this salvation was my greatest need. I was lost and needed a Saviour. I there and then accepted Christ and was saved, praise the Lord. Immediately afterwards the sick were to be prayed for. There were so many that Principal Jeffreys said he couldn't anoint them all, but if everybody who desired healing would stand up, he would pray for them all together, as they stood in the seats where they were.

" By holding on to the seat in front of me I managed to stand, then Principal Jeffreys prayed, and as he prayed something happened. I felt as if someone lifted something right off me. My whole body was charged with new life and power. My head clicked back into its place ; I was healed. My mother looked on in amazement. I wanted to sing, to shout, to dance, I even wanted to run all the way home. When I reached home I ran up the steps, I could not take time to walk, I was so happy, I took off my splint, and have never needed it since. Bless the Lord. I was healed on 11th April, 1927. My doctor could find no trace of tuberculosis. My back was perfectly straight, and I was quite well.

203

" In answer to prayer the Lord found me employment, commencing on the 2nd June, 1927.

Eleven months after the Lord healed me, I got a chill, and was taken suddenly ill. The doctor was called in ; he was afraid of bronchial pneumonia, and said this would prove whether any tuberculosis was left in my system. A request for prayer was sent to the Foursquare Gospel Church and the Lord wonderfully answered prayer by taking away every trace of chest trouble. I believe now that He only allowed that illness to come to prove that there was no tuberculosis. Shortly afterward the doctor at the Tuberculosis Dispensary sent for me and examined me. He was so amazed that he examined me twice, then he told me that I had been suffering from ' active and progressive tuberculosis of the spine,' but that I was completely cured. Praise the Lord.

" It is now over four years since the Lord healed me, and (greater miracle still) saved my soul. Eighteen months after I was saved and healed, the Lord baptised me with the Holy Ghost, thus giving me the power I so much needed to witness for Him. I do praise Him for all the way He has led me and kept me. People say, ' Are you not afraid of the disease returning ? ' Never ! I was healed by the Lord Jesus Christ Himself, and the works of His hands are perfect. He is the Great Physician, and when all others fail He never fails. I do praise God for giving me the desire to go and hear His Word being preached, and I do praise Him for those who, in these days of materialism are preaching the Gospel of the miraculous in all its fulness.

" May God bless this testimony and use it for His glory ! "

The following accounts of miraculous healing are taken from *A Ministry of the Miraculous,* by the Rev. E. C. W. Boulton. They include :

Mrs. Sivier, who was healed at Coulsdon sixteen years ago ; a little boy who was healed of epileptic fits at Forest Hill in 1926 ; and a school teacher who was healed of deafness while the Word of God was going forth at Hull in 1922.

HEALED OF RUPTURE AT COULSDON.

" I was a great sufferer and had been for years, with an internal trouble. I was also badly ruptured, so weak was I and ill that I had to be wheeled about in a bath chair. At that time I was living at Coulsdon, and Principal George Jeffreys came there to conduct a ten days' mission. I shall never forget those days. In the meeting the Principal prayed for me, the power of God came upon me and I was completely healed. The rupture disappeared, all pain departed, and I have never had a pain since.''

BOY HEALED OF EPILEPTIC FITS AT FOREST HILL.

'' One dear little lad, of very tender years, was brought by his mother to one of Principal Jeffreys' meetings at Forest Hill. For nearly three years he had suffered from epileptic fits. He had been taken to several doctors, but was pronounced incurable, as the trouble, it was stated, was of a hereditary nature. This dear child would have as many as four fits per day, and the medical verdict was that as he grew older the fits would become worse, and that he might pass away in one of them. His mother, hearing of the wonders God was doing in the district, resolved to take her boy to be prayed for. He was instantaneously healed. Mrs. Knowles adds : ' You ask me, '' Is the day of miracles past? '' My answer is, '' Hallelujah ! No ! For my little boy is a miracle !'' ' His mother describes him as ' a sturdy little boy, the picture of health.' ''

HEALED OF DEAFNESS AT HULL.

'' A further testimony of the healing virtue is that of a dear school teacher who was wonderfully healed whilst Principal Jeffreys was preaching. This took place in Hull as far back as 1922. Some years previously this sister had met with a very serious accident, in which the

206

base of the skull was fractured, and concussion of the brain resulted. A small bone was broken in the head which had punctured the drum of the left ear, rendering her stone deaf. One doctor stated that nothing less than a miracle could possibly restore the hearing. As a consequence of the accident this sister experienced severe pains in the head. It was during one of the special meetings held in Hull in 1922 that God wrought this marvellous deliverance. Without a single hand being laid upon her she was instantaneously and completely healed. She adds, ' The Lord gave me a new ear.' The Divine life filled her whole being with an unutterable glory.''

The answer to that oft-repeated question, Do healings last? is certainly found in this closing chapter, for these have stood the test of years. We might go on page after page recording the astonishing miracles of healing we have witnessed, but sufficient have been given to convince an unbiassed and unprejudiced mind. The great gatherings of the Elim Four-square revival movement in which they took place have been dominated by the all-pervading sense of Divine presence, and the power of God was present to heal. In conclusion we give the impressions by two devoted servants of Christ who have watched the progress of this revival and healing movement :

John Leech, Esq., M.A., LL.B., K.C.,

who has watched the advancement of the work from the commencement, gives the following foreword in the *Ministry of the Miraculous* :

" In the following pages of this volume, the reader will be introduced to a wonderful and thrilling account of the commencement and development of a marvellous present-day out-pouring of the Holy Spirit, and will be brought face to face with hundreds in whom the greatest of miracles, the salvation of their souls, has been wrought, as well as the instant healing of their bodies of almost every known disease. As one who has observed this work from its small beginning to its present wonderful de-velopment, I count it a privilege to testify to the wholehearted zeal of the workers, and the blessing which has accompanied their labours."

The Rev. Professor Cunningham Pike, M.A., at one time Principal of All Nations Bible College, speaking at one of our meetings, said :

" I have been on many platforms, but on none more gladly than this, for I believe you are twentieth century representatives of New Testament Christianity. This is no movement of a moment, no flash in the pan. You are pioneers going forward boldly and freely to preach and practise everything that the Bible enjoins. In sound impartial fashion the changes are rung upon the great cardinal truths. Justification by faith, holiness as a heart experience, Divine healing, the Second Advent, and the headship of Christ in the midst of the Church. Thousands of Christian people to-day are weary of cold formalism and futile rationalism ; and are looking for a living fellowship where the Bible is believed, and the Gospel preached with power. Many eyes are upon this work ; may it meet the deep and present need. Go on building on the broad, deep foundations which have already been laid with such wonderful sagacity and success.''

To God be all the glory !

Elim Publishing Co., Ltd., Park Crescent, Clapham, S.W.4.

GEORGE JEFFREYS— A MINISTRY OF THE MIRACULOUS

By E. C. W. BOULTON

A thrilling account of the birth
and growth of the Elim Work.
Four hundred pages and four
hundred photos in addition make
it worth double the price.

Cloth Boards, 2-colour jacket, **6**/- (by post 6/9)

ELIM PUBLISHING COMPANY, LIMITED,
Park Crescent, Clapham Park, London, S.W.4.

The Miraculous Foursquare Gospel

VOL. I.—DOCTRINAL.
VOL. II.—SUPERNATURAL.
(with Questions and Answers)

By Principal GEORGE JEFFREYS
(Founder and Leader of the Elim Foursquare Gospel Alliance)

Cloth Boards, **2/6** each (by post 2/10).
Paper Covers, **1/6** each (by post 1/9).

ELIM PUBLISHING COMPANY, LIMITED,
Park Crescent, Clapham Park, London, S.W.4.

CPSIA information can be obtained
at www.ICGtesting.com
Printed in the USA
BVHW08s1230261018
531296BV00005B/191/P